Until She Barely Existed

The Silent Struggle of Narcissistic Abuse

by
Tammy Eady Walker

Copyright Page

Until She Barely Existed
© 2025 Tammy Eady Walker

All rights reserved. No part of this publication may be reproduced, distributed, or transmitted in any form or by any means, including photocopying, recording, or other electronic or mechanical methods, without the prior written permission of the publisher, except in the case of brief quotations embodied in critical reviews and certain other noncommercial uses permitted by copyright law.

This is a work of fiction. Names, characters, places, and incidents are either products of the author's imagination or used fictitiously. Any resemblance to actual persons, living or dead, events, or locales is purely coincidental.

For permission requests, please contact:
Tammy Eady Walker

ISBN: 9798282653663

Printed in the United States of America
First Edition, 2025

Dedication

For every woman or man who has ever questioned their worth, doubted their strength, or felt invisible.
This story is for you.

May you always remember:
You are seen.
You are valued.
You are more powerful than you know.

With all my heart,
Tammy Eady Walker

Table of Contents Table of Contents

Dedication
Author's Note

1. The Breaking Point—1
2. How it All Began—5
3. The First Step Toward Help—11
4. The First Meeting—15
5. The Bond Begins—21
6. Cracks in the Armor—25
7. The Crumbling Façade—29
8. Michelle's Quiet Strength—33
9. One Piece at a Time—39
10. Marilyn's Story—47
11. Taryn's Knee Jerk Response—53
12. Taryn's Breaking Point—59
13. Rachel—The Good Girl—63
14. Aaron—The Apology Loop—
15. Michelle's Moment—65
16. Kyle's Crossroads—69
17. Michelle Stands Strong—73
18. The Shift—77
19. Four's a Crowd—81
20. The Unexpected Setback—85
21. Kyle's Breaking Point—89
22. Too Fast, Too Soon—93
23. Britney—The Mimic—97
24. Gina—The Door That Closed—99
25. A Taste of Freedom—105
26. Breaking Old Habits—109
27. More of the Same—113
28. Michelle Extends and Olive Branch—117
29. Alone Again, at It's Okay—121
30. The Guilt Trip—125
31. Britney's Breakthrough—129
32. Britney's New Beginning—135
33. Kyle's Turning Point—137

34. Naming the Abuse—139
35. Breaking the Silence—1
36. Slipping Back In—1
37. A New Season for Michelle—1
38. The Invitation—1
39. Shifting Ground—1
40. Michelle's Breakthrough—1
41. Kyle's Full Circle Moment—1
42. Familiar Enough to Embrace—1
43. Crossroads and Courage—1
44. When the Mask Slips—1
45. Stepping Into the Unknown—1
46. The Weight of the Past—1
47. Boundary Set, Boundary Kept—
48. A New Light—
49. The Ripples of Change—
50. Full Circle—

Epilogue—211
Resources & Support

Dedication
Author's Note

Author's Note

If you have ever felt trapped, invisible, or broken by someone who was supposed to love you, I want you to know this: **you are not alone**. So many of us have quietly carried the wounds of emotional and narcissistic abuse, feeling isolated and unseen. You might be picking up this book because something in it speaks to that hidden pain. If you see pieces of your own story reflected in the pages ahead, I am writing this introduction especially for you.

In *Until She Barely Existed*, you'll meet Taryn, a woman who appears to have a picture-perfect life from the outside. But behind closed doors, she lives in the shadows of her husband's narcissistic control—a web of manipulation, emotional cruelty, and even spiritual gaslighting that chips away at her identity piece by piece. On the surface everything seems fine; inside, she is quietly breaking. This story is a raw, honest journey through the darkness of abuse, but more importantly, it is a journey toward light, healing, and freedom.

As you read Taryn's story, you may find some moments painfully familiar. You might catch a glimpse of your own experiences in her confusion, her fear, or her hope for a way out. Some chapters could stir feelings you've kept buried. That's okay. I encourage you to take your time and remember that every feeling that surfaces—pain, anger, relief, hope—is valid. Just as Taryn finds small glimmers of hope even in her darkest moments, I want you to feel that hope too, shining through these pages.

For anyone who has ever questioned their worth, doubted their sanity, or felt trapped in a toxic relationship, I want to assure you that **healing is possible**, and you are not alone in this fight. There is a quiet strength inside you—even if you can't feel it right now—that has helped you survive each and every day. This story is, above all, a tribute to that quiet, resilient strength. Think of it as my way of reaching out to you as a friend who understands, to say that I see your struggle and I believe in your courage.

I also want to gently remind you that you don't have to walk this path by yourself. There are people and communities ready to support you and lift you up, such as:

- **A compassionate counselor or therapist:** a professional who can help you make sense of what you've been through and guide you toward healing.
- **A support group of fellow survivors:** others who have lived through similar pain, ready to listen and share their own experiences so that you realize you truly aren't alone.
- **Faith or a spiritual community:** if spirituality is important to you, a place where you can find solace, strength, and a reminder of your worth through shared hope.

Whatever form it takes, **support is out there**, and you deserve to receive it.

I know that reaching out for help—or even admitting you need it—can be one of the hardest steps to take. When you've been hurt deeply, trusting anyone (or even your own voice) might feel impossible. But I encourage you, when you are ready, to take that first brave step toward healing. Whether it's making a phone call to a therapist, confiding in a trusted friend or family member, joining a support group, or saying a small prayer for strength—each of these is a courageous step forward. **You have carried this pain long enough**, and you deserve to find peace and reclaim the life and happiness that belong to you.

As you begin this story, please know that *Until She Barely Existed* was written with the utmost love, empathy, and hope. It's okay to pause if you need to, to breathe, and to remind yourself that you're reading in a safe space. My greatest wish is that through Taryn's journey, you will see a reflection of your own strength and the promise of brighter days ahead. You are not broken beyond repair, and you are never truly alone.

Thank you for being here and for giving Taryn's story a chance. I am honored to share it with you. Above all, I want you to remember: there is hope, there is help, and you deserve every bit of healing and happiness to come.

With love and hope,
Tammy Eady Walker

Chapter 1

The Breaking Point

Taryn sat in disbelief. She couldn't fully explain what was happening—it was unsettling yet eerily familiar, like slipping back into a pattern she'd sworn she'd never repeat. She sat alone in the car, stunned, asking herself the same question she always did: *How did I allow this to happen again?*

As much as she grieved, she knew deep down this was the way it had always been. And heartbreakingly, she also knew this was likely how it would always be. There was nothing she could do to change it. She told herself over and over, *This is not right. This is not how a marriage is supposed to be. This is not how a man should treat his wife.*

Pete had yelled at her—and at the kids—the entire way to church. She couldn't even remember what had sparked his fury this time. She sat there retracing every step of the morning, every word spoken, grasping for the trigger. But the truth was, there was never really a reason. No matter how carefully she tiptoed or how perfectly she followed the unspoken rules, it was never enough. The same old question burned in her heart: *Why?*

But there was never a *why*.

Why was the same old, unanswered question.

And yet…

"And so she stayed. And so she endured. Until she barely existed."

She walked into the church building several steps behind her husband, though not intentionally. Pete always walked ahead of her—it was his personal power move, like he was racing to win something. The moment the car was parked, he bolted across the lot, never once looking back to see where Taryn was or how she was managing. He didn't care. This was his element. He was about to put on his best performance of the week.

He was in God's house—*"God's holy and glorious house."*

"Welcome," said the woman at the door, smiling brightly.

Taryn made her way toward the coffee stand and poured herself a cup of hot water. As she reached for a tea bag, a woman she didn't recognize bumped into her, acting as though they were old friends.

"Oh, hello there! You're Pete's wife, right? Oh, you have such an amazing husband! He's so helpful and friendly. My husband ushers with him and just loves Pete. You are so blessed to have such a wonderful husband. What a true servant's heart he has."

Taryn forced a smile. "Um… yes, I'm really blessed," she replied, her voice calm, her smile polite, as she reached for the sugar.

She didn't dare say more. She knew the game. She'd played it for years. But a quiet thought flitted through her mind: *What if I said something different? What if I told her the truth?*

But no, she'd been down that road before and knew exactly where it led—a dead end. So she nodded and listened as the woman continued with light chatter—*"church chat,"* as Taryn called it.

She used to love church. She loved God with all her heart. Just the night before, she had cried out to Him, begging for strength to carry this burden, praying for wisdom to "defuse" Pete's next rampage. But the game—the exhausting, never-ending game—had worn her down. After more than 20 years of playing it, her soul had silently cried "Uncle."

She didn't know this woman. They hadn't been attending this church long. Over the years, they had cycled through seven different churches. Pete always seemed to "hear from the Spirit" that it was time to leave—usually right around the time the church leaders started treating him differently. According to Pete, it was because the leaders "didn't allow him to serve where he was called." So, they'd move on.

This church? They'd left it twice before, but now "the Spirit" told Pete it was time to return.

The endless moving made Taryn cautious. She no longer allowed herself to form deep connections. What was the point? The moment a place started feeling like home, they'd uproot again. Two churches ago, she had joined a quilting group—a wonderful circle of women. They shared projects, visited each other's homes, and built something real. For a brief moment, she felt community.

Pete didn't like it.

Pete did not like any of her friends. He criticized every friend she brought home, insisting they were unhealthy or needy. He'd complain that she never chose the right kinds of friends—why couldn't she connect with the pastor's wife or other church leaders? Even her long-time friends from before their marriage weren't spared his scrutiny. Eventually, to avoid conflict, she stopped bringing anyone home and, little by little, stepped away from the quilting group altogether.

As she stirred her tea, her gaze drifted to a bulletin board advertising a local support group: *"Finding Freedom: Healing for the Wounded Soul. Thursdays at 7 PM."* She lingered on the flyer longer than she meant to.

Taryn secured the lid on her tea and started toward the foyer, where others were gathering to enter the sanctuary. A dull ache throbbed in her left knee, something she'd been ignoring for days. Pete strolled over and, loud enough to make heads turn, called out:

"Hello Beautiful."

With a bounce in his step, Pete led the way inside. He spotted one of his usher friends and greeted him with an enthusiastic hug. Then, turning to Taryn and gesturing grandly with both hands, he said loudly:

"Isn't she just the most beautiful woman you have ever seen?"

She gave a quick nod, her face neutral.

Taryn's stomach tightened. This wasn't about her. It never was. What was that poor man supposed to say? *How* was he supposed to answer such a ridiculous question?

Thankfully, the people started moving towards their seats. This time, Taryn made a deliberate choice—she walked several steps ahead of Pete. It was a small move. This was her "take back a bit of power" move.

It was all the power she had.

But, it was power, none the less.

Chapter 2

How It All Began

In the beginning, Taryn never imagined her life would turn out like this.

She was 28 when she met Pete, a single mom raising her four-year-old son, Brandon. She was fiercely independent, managing a tight household on her own, and proud of the little family she'd built. Life wasn't easy—never had been—but it was hers, and she made the decisions.

They met at a friend's backyard barbecue. Pete had that kind of magnetic charm that turned heads the moment he entered a room—tall, polished, quick with a smile. Taryn wasn't looking for love—she'd sworn off men after Brandon's father abandoned them—but Pete locked eyes with her across the yard, and something about his attention felt... disarming.

"You're Taryn, right? Brandon's mom?" he asked, smiling.

She nodded, caught off guard by his confidence.

"I've heard you're one of the strongest women around," he added smoothly. The words hit a tender place she didn't realize was exposed. Compliments like that were rare, and Pete delivered them with practiced ease.

Within a month, they were dating. Pete was attentive in ways Taryn had never experienced: flowers at work, surprise dinners, and—most captivating of all—genuine interest in Brandon. Or at least, it seemed genuine.

"I want to be a father to him," Pete said one evening as they sat side by side on her old couch, Brandon sleeping upstairs. "He deserves a good man in his life."

It felt like an answer to years of lonely prayers. After holding everything together on her own for so long, Taryn couldn't believe her luck. They married a year later in a modest church ceremony. Taryn wore a simple white dress, Pete stood tall in his suit, and Brandon beamed as Pete vowed to love them both forever.

For a while, it was perfect. Pete showered her with praise and affection, telling anyone who would listen how blessed he was. He joined church committees, led Bible studies, and seemed to thrive as the picture-perfect husband. Taryn felt proud—finally, she'd found her real family.

But it didn't last.

The cracks appeared slowly, almost imperceptibly. Pete didn't like her best friend, Angela, and started urging her to see less of her. He criticized her clothes—"That skirt's a little too short for church, don't you think?"—and subtly inserted himself into every decision. His praise became conditional. His smiles grew tight.

When their son Kenny was born two years later followed by their daughter Kate a year after that, the pressure ramped up. Pete insisted she quit her job to be a full-time mom. "It's God's design," he said. Taryn, exhausted and eager to be the perfect wife, agreed—without realizing the isolation had just begun.

Brandon was now away at college. He would call home from time to time and always ask to talk to Kenny and Kate but other than that he was off living his best life. Taryn was proud of the great man he was becoming.

Pete's moods turned volatile. He was the model husband in public, lavishing her with compliments and affection at church, but at home, his words cut deep. She never knew which Pete she would face: the doting partner or the cruel critic. He called her lazy, ungrateful, and spiritually broken.

"You're not the godly woman I thought you were," he hissed during fights. "You have an evil spirit in you. You're controlled by the devil. I deserve better."

It became a cycle: verbal attacks, silent treatments, fake apologies. Pete was a master manipulator, and Taryn was exhausted. She learned to read the warning signs—the clenched jaw, the too-quiet stare—and taught Kenny and Kate to tread lightly. Their house wasn't a home. It was a stage, with Pete always playing the lead.

And then came moments that felt like straight-up madness.

Like the day before Kate's spring dance recital. Taryn was in the kitchen making cupcakes, she went looking for the frosting she'd bought the day before—a special can with a squirt nozzle. But when she reached into the pantry, it was gone.

She searched every shelf, puzzled, until finally she asked, "Pete, have you seen the chocolate frosting?"

No answer.

She tried again. "Pete, I know I bought it. Did you move it?"

Still nothing.

A third time, more insistent: "Pete? Where's the frosting?"

Suddenly, Pete exploded. "Why do you care about your stupid cupcakes? Why don't you care about God? You never read your Bible. You never pray!"

"I pray every day," she said calmly.

"I never hear you."

"God hears me."

Pete stormed off, slamming the bedroom door. And then came the **wall talk**—his trademark move. Loud, bitter lectures, meant for her ears but disguised as prayers.

"Oh Lord, why did You curse me with such a horrible wife? She's so mean and ungodly. Why won't she submit like a good Christian woman?"

Taryn stood frozen, her stomach churning.

An hour later, when she came back downstairs, there it was: the missing can of frosting, sitting on the table. And beside it, scrawled in frosting: "Dumb Bitch."

She stared in disbelief. After everything, this felt... childish. Petty. Yet another line crossed.

She snapped a photo and walked out of the house, leaving the mess behind. Driving aimlessly, she gripped the wheel and whispered to herself: *One day soon, I'm leaving for good.*

But the madness didn't end there.

That night, exhausted, she ordered her kids' favorite pizzas from Pizza Place—pepperoni and combo. When Pete came in, she mentioned, "Pizza's on the way."

"From where?" he asked.

"Pizza Place."

"I hope not. I hate their pizza," he sneered.

"It's already ordered."

Twenty minutes later, the doorbell rang. Taryn set the pizzas on the table, relieved the night was winding down. But five minutes later, Pete walked in holding a pizza box—from a *different* restaurant.

He made a show of it, lifting the lid with exaggerated flair. "Oh man, you don't want that garbage your mom ordered. Here, Kenny—try this. Way better."

The kids giggled, caught up in the performance. Pete grinned, trashing Taryn's pizza loudly, turning it into a game.

Crazy making. Pure and simple. He lived for it.

And Taryn? She became an expert in survival. She tiptoed around his moods, teaching the kids to stay quiet, always bracing for the next storm.

By the time the kids were born, the cycles were ingrained. Pete's manipulation deepened. He twisted scripture to tighten his grip, making Taryn believe she was failing—not just as a wife and mother, but as a Christian.

And yet… she stayed.

Looking back, sitting in her car after another tense church service, Taryn's eyes welled up. How much of her life had she spent simply enduring?

She looked at the card she had picked up at church the Sunday before. It had the name of a therapist, Marilyn Carter. On the back it read: **Finding Freedom.** The words felt laughably distant. But still, something stirred inside her. Maybe… just maybe… it was time to try.

Chapter 3

The First Step Toward Help

Taryn sat in the waiting room, nervously tapping her foot against the tiled floor. The faint hum of an air purifier filled the silence, and a small tabletop fountain trickled in the corner. It was her first session with Marilyn—the therapist Angela had quietly recommended after church one day.

Taryn wasn't sure what to expect. Part of her didn't even believe therapy could help. She had kept her pain locked up for so long that the idea of unpacking it with a stranger felt both terrifying and... oddly hopeful.

"Hi, Taryn?" Marilyn's voice was gentle but confident as she appeared at the door, clipboard in hand. "Come on in."

The office was warm and inviting. Not clinical, not intimidating—just shelves of books, a few plush chairs, and a table with a small basket of tissues placed thoughtfully nearby. Taryn hesitated for a moment before sitting down.

"So," Marilyn began after some small talk, "what brings you here today?"

Taryn hesitated. She knew the answer but couldn't seem to form the words. Finally, she offered the only thing she felt safe admitting: "I don't even know where to start. I just... I feel like I'm disappearing. Like the person I once was barely exists anymore."

Marilyn nodded, patient and unrushed. "That's a powerful place to start."

And so, week after week, Taryn came back. At first, she talked about surface things—stress, exhaustion, church. But Marilyn had a gift for gently guiding her deeper, peeling back layers Taryn didn't even realize were there. Over time, bits of truth began to tumble out: Pete's temper. His unpredictable moods. His sharp words that cut deep and left scars no one could see.

One day, after Taryn had recounted a particularly brutal verbal tirade from Pete, she noticed Marilyn's quiet pause. "Taryn," Marilyn said gently, "has anyone ever used the word 'abuse' when talking about your marriage?"

Taryn froze. She felt like she'd been slapped. The word hung heavy in the room.

"I... I don't know," Taryn whispered. "Is that really what this is?"

Marilyn leaned forward slightly. "I want you to know that emotional, verbal, spiritual, and even physical abuse can be subtle at first. It chips away at you little by little until one day you wake up and realize you don't recognize yourself anymore."

Tears spilled down Taryn's cheeks before she could stop them. "That's exactly how I feel," she sobbed. "I don't even know who I am anymore."

Marilyn handed her a tissue, her voice steady but full of compassion. "You are still in there, Taryn. And you are stronger than you realize."

As the weeks passed, Taryn grew bolder in sharing her truth. She described the isolation, the constant moves from church to church, Pete's dismissive attitude toward her friends, and his habit of twisting scripture into weapons. She even began, tentatively, to mention some of the physical incidents—though shame and fear still made her hesitant to tell the full story.

One afternoon, after Taryn shared a moment of deep vulnerability, Marilyn spoke softly. "I want to tell you about something that has helped other women in your situation. I lead a support group—Thursday nights. It's a safe space where women who've experienced similar dynamics come together. You don't have to talk if you don't want to. You can just sit and listen until you're ready."

Taryn bit her lip. The idea of sitting in a room with strangers, admitting her secrets, sent a fresh wave of anxiety through her.

"I don't know..." she whispered. "What if... what if people judge me? What if I can't handle it?"

Marilyn smiled, a reassuring warmth in her eyes. "That's the beautiful thing, Taryn. You'll be sitting with women who already understand—women who've lived it, too. There's no judgment. Just support."

For the first time in a long time, Taryn felt a flicker of something she hadn't allowed herself to feel in years: hope. Maybe—just maybe—there was a path out of the darkness.

She wiped her tears and nodded slowly. "Okay. I'll think about it."

And over the next few days, that small seed Marilyn planted began to take root. Taryn kept hearing the words in her mind: *You are still in there... and you are stronger than you realize.*

A week later, she picked up her phone and texted Marilyn: *Is there room for me at group this Thursday?*

The reply came almost immediately: *Always.*

Chapter 4

The First Meeting

It was a gray Thursday evening, the kind of evening where everything felt a little heavier—like the sky itself was pressing down. Taryn sat in her car, engine off, fingers gripping the steering wheel until her knuckles were white. The church basement loomed ahead, not menacing exactly, but unfamiliar.

She glanced at the worn flyer on the passenger seat, the words nearly memorized now: *Finding Freedom: Healing for the Wounded Soul. Thursdays at 7 PM. Led by Marilyn Carter, licensed therapist.* Taryn now realizing this was the same group she had seen the flyer for at church.

Taryn had tucked that flyer into her purse over a month ago, after one of her appointments with Marilyn. She had even picked it up once, only to bury it under bills and grocery lists at home. But tonight—tonight felt different. Or maybe *she* was different.

You don't belong here, her inner critic whispered. *Other people need this. You're fine. Besides, what if someone sees you?*

She almost started the car back up. Almost. But then, as if moved by something beyond herself, she found her hand reaching for the door handle. Before she could talk herself out of it, her feet hit the pavement.

She pulled her coat tight around her and walked toward the church's side entrance, heart pounding. Her knee ached—her old injury flaring as if reminding her why she was here in the first place.

Inside, the building smelled faintly of coffee and cleaning solution. She found the meeting room downstairs: a simple space with folding chairs in a circle, a small table with coffee and store-bought cookies, and a handful of people settling in.

Marilyn spotted her from a distance and her smile deepened. "Welcome, Taryn. So glad you're here. No pressure at all—just sit wherever you feel comfortable."

Taryn slid into a seat near the edge of the circle, clutching a cup of tea she didn't really want. She scanned the room quickly, avoiding eye contact but taking them all in: about ten people, a mix of men and women, all looking equally guarded.

Across from her sat a man, maybe late 30s, with a kind but tired face and a baseball cap pulled low. He seemed to keep fidgeting, eyes darting around the room. His name tag said Kyle.

Next to him was a woman with dark, shoulder-length hair and a soft, almost fragile demeanor. She kept her hands folded tightly in her lap, her eyes down. *Michelle,* her tag read.

Taryn's eyes swept across others: Gina, who looked sharp and fierce even though her eyes hinted at sadness; Rachel, younger but visibly tense; Aaron, quiet and closed-off, his arms folded across his chest. And at the edge of the circle, a younger woman—Britney—wearing oversized sunglasses indoors, glancing at her phone every few minutes.

Marilyn clapped her hands gently. "Let's settle in. Tonight, we're talking about something many of you have likely faced: gaslighting and emotional manipulation. Sometimes, it's the invisible wounds that cut the deepest."

She spoke for a while about the classic signs—how abusers shift blame, rewrite history, minimize your reality until you question your own sanity. Every word hit Taryn like a stone in her gut. She wasn't imagining things. She *wasn't crazy.*

When Marilyn invited people to share, there was a pause. Then Kyle cleared his throat. "I'll go. My wife, Sidney... she's... well, let's just say, she's got a way of making me feel like I'm the crazy one. I catch her in lies, and somehow I'm the problem. She, uh... she's cheated on me more than once. Promises she'll change. Never does."

He let out a bitter laugh. "But I keep going back. Like a fool."

Marilyn nodded gently. "Thank you, Kyle. That takes courage to say."

Next was Michelle, her voice so soft Taryn leaned in to hear. "My husband, Matt, controls... everything. I stopped working because he said it was best for the kids. But now... I don't even have access to a bank account. I get... an allowance, if you can call it that. I feel... trapped. Like I don't even exist sometimes."

Gina piped up next, her tone sharper. "Mine's a charmer. The nicest guy in the world—until you disagree with him. Then it's like flipping a switch. And everyone thinks I'm the problem because he's so good at the act."

Others shared too, little glimpses of their pain spilling into the room. Taryn's chest tightened with every word, feeling their stories weave into hers like threads of the same fabric.

And then it was her turn. She hesitated, her heart pounding in her ears. But something inside—some tiny flicker of rebellion—pushed her forward.

"I'm Taryn," she began. Her voice trembled. "And... my husband is one of those people everyone admires. At church, at work—he's... respected. They think he's this... godly man. But at home...

it's different. The things he says, the way he... twists things... I don't even recognize myself anymore."

Her breath caught. "I... I used to be strong. But now... I just feel... hollow."

Marilyn's eyes were full of quiet understanding. "Thank you, Taryn. That's incredibly brave."

The room fell silent for a moment. And in that silence, something remarkable happened: Taryn felt... seen. Not pitied, not judged—just... seen.

After the meeting, people began filing out, murmuring their goodbyes. Taryn lingered near the door, unsure what to do next.

"Hey," a voice said. She turned to see Kyle, holding his coat, offering a tentative smile. "A few of us usually head over to *The Corner Table* for coffee after these meetings. No pressure, but... you're welcome to join."

Michelle appeared beside him, nodding shyly. "It's... nice to decompress a bit."

Taryn hesitated. The old her—the obedient, always-rushing-home Taryn—would have politely declined. But tonight, she was tired of that voice.

"I'd like that," she heard herself say.

The coffee shop was small and cozy, its yellow glow spilling onto the sidewalk like a welcome mat. They found a booth near the back, ordered steaming mugs of coffee and slices of pie—cherry, lemon meringue, and coconut cream—and settled in.

At first, it was awkward. But as the minutes ticked by, their stories began spilling out more easily. Kyle talked about Sidney's endless betrayals and how he still couldn't bring himself to leave. Michelle shared how she clipped coupons just to have pocket change because Matt controlled every dime.

And Taryn... Taryn found herself opening up in ways she hadn't in years. She told them about Pete's charm, his rages, the way he prayed out loud as if God were his personal audience. She even laughed—a real, surprised laugh—when she told them about the pizza incident and the ridiculousness of Pete's passive-aggressive stunts.

They all laughed with her—not at her, but with the knowing laugh of people who'd lived it too.

That night, as she climbed into bed beside Pete—who grunted something unintelligible and rolled over—Taryn felt something different.

Hope.

Fragile, yes. But there. And for the first time in a long time, she whispered a prayer not of desperation... but of thanks.

Thank you, God... for leading me there tonight.

Chapter 5

The Bond Begins

The next Thursday came faster than Taryn expected. All week, she'd replayed moments from the group meeting and coffee afterward—snippets of laughter, raw admissions, the unmistakable comfort of *being understood.*

Pete, oblivious as always, hadn't noticed anything different. If anything, he was in one of his "good phases," full of fake cheerfulness and dramatic prayers over dinner. But beneath it all, Taryn felt changed. A tiny, almost imperceptible shift—but a shift nonetheless.

When Thursday arrived, she left early under the same excuse—Bible study—and parked in her usual spot outside the church basement. Her heart still pounded as she walked in, but this time it was mingled with something new: anticipation.

Inside, the same circle of chairs waited. Kyle and Michelle were already there, chatting quietly in the corner. Kyle spotted her first, waving her over with a grin.

"Hey! Look who's back."

Michelle smiled shyly. "I'm glad you came."

Taryn felt warmth spread through her chest. *Me too,* she thought.

Soon, the others trickled in. Gina, with her fiery gaze; Rachel, clutching a worn journal; Aaron, as guarded as ever. And Britney, who breezed in wearing oversized sunglasses again, taking her usual spot near the edge.

Marilyn welcomed everyone with her signature calm. "Tonight's topic," she began, "is about boundary setting. For many of us who've endured cycles of abuse, boundaries feel... foreign. Or even selfish. But they are essential to healing."

She passed out handouts outlining examples of healthy boundaries—things like, *'I am not responsible for others' happiness,'* and, *'I have the right to say no without guilt.'*

Taryn read the list with disbelief. The words felt revolutionary, like glimpses into a world she'd never dared imagine for herself.

When sharing time came, Gina spoke up first, her voice steady. "I've been working on boundaries for years," she admitted. "It's... hard. My ex would blow up whenever I tried. But I've learned that his reaction isn't my responsibility. I still struggle with guilt, though."

Kyle was next. "Boundaries? I suck at those," he said with a laugh. "Sidney crosses every line, and I just... let her. I guess I'm afraid if I push back, she'll leave. And even though I know I should want that, part of me... doesn't."

Michelle's voice trembled. "I... don't even know what a boundary looks like. Matt decides everything. I'm... scared of what would happen if I stood up to him."

Taryn listened, her heart aching at how familiar it all sounded. Finally, she found her voice. "I've... never really set boundaries either. Every time I tried, Pete would either explode or turn it into a guilt trip. After a while, I just... stopped trying. It felt safer that way."

Marilyn nodded. "That's very common. But remember—boundaries aren't about controlling others. They're about protecting *yourself*."

As the meeting wrapped up, Taryn felt a growing sense of connection—not just with Kyle and Michelle, but with the group as a whole. Even Britney, who barely spoke, seemed to soften a little when Marilyn offered closing thoughts.

Outside, Kyle turned to Taryn and Michelle. "Same plan as last week? Coffee?"

Michelle hesitated. "I... really shouldn't spend money..."

"Nonsense," Kyle said, waving her off. "My treat tonight. Come on—you deserve it."

Michelle smiled, and Taryn felt her own grin stretch wider. Together, they walked down the street to *The Corner Table,* sliding into their now-familiar booth near the back.

Kyle ordered a giant slice of cherry pie and coffee for everyone. Michelle, shy at first, eventually let herself relax, and they spent over an hour talking about everything from silly pet peeves to their worst "crazy-making" moments.

"Sidney once hid my car keys when I was late for work," Kyle said, shaking his head. "I found them two days later... in the freezer."

Taryn laughed. "Oh, I get that. Pete once hid a can of frosting I needed for Kate's school cupcakes. Then left me a message with frosting on the table that said... well, something too awful to repeat."

Michelle's eyes widened. "That's... unbelievable."

"Nope. Sadly, it's real," Taryn said. "And he did it with a straight face."

They laughed—not because it was funny, but because laughter was the only way to keep from crying.

By the time they left the coffee shop, something had shifted between them. The walls were coming down. This wasn't just a group of strangers anymore. It was starting to feel like... family.

As they said their goodbyes, Kyle grinned. "Same time next week?"

Michelle smiled. "Yeah. I'd... like that."

Taryn felt the same flicker of hope she'd felt last week, but stronger now. A little light in the dark.

And as she drove home, she whispered again, *Thank you, God. For this little glimpse of freedom.*

She didn't know it yet, but this was only the beginning.

Chapter 6

Cracks in the Armor

The weeks began to pass in a rhythm Taryn hadn't expected. Every Thursday night was like oxygen—those precious few hours when she could step outside the suffocating confines of her marriage and breathe freely. The group became her lifeline. And Kyle and Michelle? They were no longer just coffee companions; they were her tribe.

Tonight's meeting was different, though. There was a heavier energy in the room, as if everyone had carried extra weight through the door.

Marilyn began as always, with a calm, grounding voice. "Tonight's topic is 'Crazy-Making'—a tactic often used by narcissists and abusers to keep you doubting your own reality."

Taryn leaned forward. *Crazy-making.* She knew that term too well. Even the name made her stomach twist.

Marilyn continued, "It can look like hiding things, denying things they said or did, making you feel irrational for having emotions. Over time, it can erode your sense of reality."

Kyle let out a low laugh. "That hits close to home already."

Marilyn smiled gently. "I'd love to hear your stories tonight—whatever you feel comfortable sharing."

Kyle was the first to jump in. "Sidney is a master at it. I'll confront her about something she said, and she'll swear I imagined it. One time, she actually made me apologize for getting upset about something *she* did. And... I did. I actually apologized."

Taryn nodded along, feeling the knot in her stomach tighten. "Pete does that too. He hides things. I mean, literally hides things—car keys, my phone, even food in the pantry—then acts like I'm losing my mind when I can't find them. He twists everything until I don't even trust my own memory."

Michelle spoke next, her hands twisting the fabric of her sweater. "Matt... he's quieter about it. But he'll act like my feelings don't matter at all. If I cry, he'll say I'm 'too emotional.' If I bring up a concern, he'll say I'm 'overthinking.' I've stopped mentioning things because... what's the point?"

Rachel, who'd been mostly silent in previous meetings, chimed in with a shaky voice. "Mine tells me I'm the crazy one. He even said once that I should be locked up. For a while... I started to believe it."

The room went still. No one rushed to fill the silence—there was something sacred in letting those words settle.

Marilyn finally spoke. "Crazy-making is one of the most damaging forms of abuse because it targets your mind. But I want you all to hear this: *Your reality matters. Your feelings matter.* You are not crazy."

Taryn felt tears sting her eyes. How many years had she wondered if she was the problem? How many nights had she prayed for clarity, for some kind of proof that she wasn't as broken as Pete made her out to be?

The meeting wrapped with Marilyn encouraging them to practice one thing this week: *writing down incidents in a journal.* "When your reality is challenged, your own written words can help ground you," she said.

As they filed out, Kyle caught Taryn and Michelle at the door. "Coffee?"

Michelle hesitated. "I really should get home..."

"Just one cup," Kyle urged. "Come on. We need pie after tonight."

Taryn smiled. "I'm in."

Michelle laughed softly. "Okay. One cup."

At *The Corner Table,* they settled into their booth, the comfort of routine washing over them. This time, Kyle ordered a ridiculous slice of peanut butter chocolate pie, and they all laughed as it nearly toppled over on his plate.

"So," Kyle said, digging in, "is it just me, or does this journaling thing sound... kind of terrifying?"

Michelle nodded. "I feel the same. It's like... if I write it down, it becomes too real."

Taryn sipped her tea. "But maybe that's the point. I've been gaslit so much I don't even trust my own memories half the time. I think... I need to see it in black and white."

Kyle stared into his coffee. "Yeah. Same."

They sat in comfortable silence for a moment, each lost in their own thoughts.

Finally, Michelle spoke, her voice tentative. "You know... I've been thinking about leaving."

Kyle and Taryn both looked up sharply.

Michelle blushed. "Not right away. But... I've been researching jobs. Teaching jobs. I miss working. I miss... me."

Taryn reached across the table and squeezed her hand. "That's huge, Michelle."

Kyle's eyes shone with pride. "You'd be an amazing teacher again."

Michelle looked down, her voice barely a whisper. "It's scary. But... I think I'm ready to start planning."

They sat with that, the weight of her words settling like something sacred.

Then Kyle grinned. "Hey, maybe when we all leave, we should just rent a place together. Be like... codependent roommates."

Taryn laughed. "We'd need a giant fridge for all the pie."

Michelle giggled, wiping her eyes. "We'd be... unstoppable."

They laughed, but deep down, each of them was wondering: *What if? What if we really could break free?*

That night, as Taryn drove home, her knee aching and her mind spinning, she felt something new bubbling under the surface.

Determination.

It was faint, but it was there. And maybe—just maybe—it was enough to get her through another week.

Chapter 7

The Crumbling Façade

Taryn sat at her kitchen table, staring blankly at a spreadsheet on her laptop. Her fingers hovered over the keyboard, but her mind was a million miles away. Pete had stormed out an hour earlier after accusing her of being "lazy" and "selfish" for not folding the laundry fast enough.

She exhaled slowly. The air in the house felt heavy, thick with tension even in his absence. Her knee throbbed—another flare-up from the injury that seemed to ache more when her stress was high.

She reached for her journal, the one Marilyn had encouraged them all to start. At first, she'd been hesitant. But after last week's meeting, she forced herself to begin.

She flipped to a fresh page and started writing:

Today, Pete hid my keys again. I know it was him. He pretended to "find" them under the couch cushions, but I had already checked there. He called me forgetful and said I'm losing my mind. I told him I'd looked there twice. He smirked.

She stopped, staring at the words. Seeing it in ink made it feel... undeniable. Real. For so long, she'd brushed things off, convinced herself she was overreacting. But this? This was proof.

Her phone buzzed—a text from Michelle.

Michelle: *Thinking of you today. Hope you're okay.*

Taryn smiled. She quickly typed back.

Taryn: *Thanks, friend. Rough day. But your text helped more than you know.*

It struck her how little kindness she'd been shown in her own home. How strange—and beautiful—it felt to be checked on, seen, without strings attached.

Later that evening, as Pete sulked in the living room, muttering bitter prayers under his breath, Taryn slipped out, claiming she needed to pick up groceries. Instead, she drove to a quiet parking lot near the water and sat in the dark with her windows down, just... breathing.

Her phone rang—Kyle.

"Hey," she answered, surprised.

"Hey," he said, his voice low and tired. "I just... needed to talk to someone. Sidney's at it again."

Taryn leaned back in her seat. "What happened?"

"She blew up because I wouldn't give her money for some spa weekend. Told me I'm worthless. That she deserves better. The usual."

Taryn's heart ached for him. "I'm so sorry, Kyle."

He let out a bitter laugh. "You ever wonder if we're just... stuck? Like, no matter what we do, we end up in the same place?"

"All the time," Taryn admitted quietly.

They sat in silence, the hum of the night filling the space between them.

"Thanks for answering," Kyle said eventually. "I didn't know who else to call."

"I'm glad you did," Taryn said. "We've got each other's backs, remember?"

"Yeah," he said softly. "We do."

When Taryn hung up, she sat for a long moment, staring out at the water. She thought about Michelle, bravely researching teaching jobs. About Kyle, caught in the same endless loop. And about herself—sitting in a car alone, hiding from the man she married.

She opened her journal again and wrote:

I deserve better. We all do. But knowing it and believing it are two different things. One day... I hope to believe it.

Thursday Night Group

The next meeting had a different energy. Marilyn welcomed them as always, but tonight she introduced a new concept: *trauma bonding.*

"Trauma bonding is when the cycles of abuse create emotional attachment," Marilyn explained. "The highs and lows, the moments of love followed by cruelty—it traps you. Even when you know the relationship is toxic, breaking free feels impossible."

Taryn's chest tightened. She glanced at Kyle and Michelle—both nodding, eyes down.

Marilyn added, "Tonight, I want us to share examples of when we've felt *stuck,* even when we knew better."

Michelle spoke first. "Matt can be so cruel. But when he apologizes... when he's suddenly sweet again... it's like I forget everything bad. For a little while, I believe things will be different. Even though they never are."

Kyle's jaw tightened. "Sid's the same. She'll cheat, scream, tear me down... and then, out of nowhere, she's crying, saying I'm the love of her life. And I fall for it. Every time."

Taryn felt her hands trembling. She took a deep breath. "Pete does this thing... after he's been horrible, he'll go into what I call his 'saint mode.' He'll do the dishes, bring me tea, pray out loud... like nothing ever happened. And for a minute, I think maybe it's over. Maybe this time..."

Her voice broke, and Marilyn stepped in. "That's the trauma bond at work. It's not your fault. It's a survival mechanism. But recognizing it is the first step to breaking free."

Afterward, at *The Corner Table,* they sat in their usual booth, the comfort of routine now like a warm blanket.

"I hate how true that all was," Kyle said, shaking his head. "It's like... we're addicted."

Michelle nodded. "But I'm starting to see it more clearly now. That's something, right?"

Taryn smiled weakly. "It's everything."

Kyle raised his coffee mug. "To seeing things clearly—even when it hurts."

They clinked mugs, a silent promise hanging in the air.

Chapter 8

Michelle's Quiet Strength

The air was crisp and sharp as Taryn stepped out of her car and pulled her coat tighter. She'd arrived early at the church basement that evening, something she hadn't done before, and was surprised to find Michelle already there, sitting on a bench outside the entrance.

Michelle looked up and smiled faintly, hugging her purse to her chest. Her eyes were tired, but there was something else too—an edge of determination that Taryn hadn't seen before.

"Hey," Taryn said, settling beside her. "You're early."

Michelle nodded. "Yeah. I... needed to be out of the house."

They sat in comfortable silence for a moment, watching the evening sky shift from pale blue to deep gray.

"How are things?" Taryn asked gently.

Michelle let out a breath, visible in the cold air. "Rough. Matt's been... worse lately. Controlling. Dismissive. But... I applied for a job today."

Taryn's eyes widened. "Michelle! That's incredible."

Michelle smiled, a little shyly. "It's just a teaching position at a small private school. But... it's a start. I don't know if I'll even get an interview, but... it felt good. To do something for me."

Taryn squeezed her hand. "I'm so proud of you."

Michelle's eyes glistened. "Thanks. I don't think I could have even *thought* about it without you and Kyle. This group... it's changed everything."

Before Taryn could respond, the door opened and Marilyn poked her head out, smiling. "Ladies! Come on in. The kettle's hot."

Inside, the group trickled in as usual. Kyle arrived a few minutes late, hair damp from the rain, and slid into a seat next to Taryn and Michelle.

"Sorry," he muttered. "Sid locked my keys in the car. Or, well... 'accidentally' locked them, as she claims."

Taryn and Michelle exchanged a knowing glance.

Tonight, Marilyn's lesson was on **"Minimizing and Deflection."**

"Narcissistic abusers often downplay your feelings," she explained, "making you feel silly, overdramatic, or selfish for having normal emotions. They'll also deflect blame, twisting situations to make it seem like *you're* the one at fault."

Taryn nodded slowly. *This hit home. Hard.*

Marilyn asked the group to share moments when their feelings had been minimized.

Rachel went first this time. "Whenever I cry, my boyfriend tells me I'm 'too sensitive.' Like... as if that makes my hurt feelings invalid. He says I'm blowing things out of proportion, even when he's been outright cruel."

Aaron spoke quietly. "My dad used to do that too. Every time I brought up something that hurt me, he'd say I was 'being dramatic' or that I needed to 'toughen up.' Now, my wife does the same thing."

Kyle sighed. "Sid's favorite line is, 'You're making something out of nothing.' Every. Single. Time. Even when she's blatantly wrong, she'll twist it until I'm questioning if I imagined the whole thing."

Michelle's voice was soft but steady. "Matt... he tells me I'm selfish if I express any kind of need. If I say I'm tired or overwhelmed, he says, 'What do *you* have to be stressed about? You don't even work.' It makes me feel... invisible."

The room was quiet for a moment, everyone absorbing the weight of those words.

Finally, Taryn spoke. "Pete tells me I'm not a 'real Christian' when I get upset. He says godly women don't complain, don't cry, don't question their husbands. He has even gone as far as telling me I am controlled by the devil. He uses my faith to shame me into silence."

Marilyn nodded, her eyes kind. "That's spiritual abuse layered on top of emotional abuse. It's insidious—and so damaging. I'm proud of each of you for recognizing these patterns. That's a huge step toward breaking free."

As the meeting wrapped up, Marilyn handed out small slips of paper. "Homework this week: Write down one boundary you plan to set. It can be small. But it's a step toward reclaiming your voice."

At The Corner Table

The familiar coffee shop felt like a sanctuary that night. The three of them claimed their booth, ordered coffee and pie—apple crumble this time—and settled in.

Michelle was the first to speak. "I want to share my boundary idea."

Taryn and Kyle leaned in, curious.

Michelle straightened her shoulders. "I'm going to tell Matt that from now on, I'll be handling my own spending money. Even if it's just grocery money... I want control over *something*."

Taryn's eyes shone. "That's amazing, Michelle."

Kyle raised his coffee mug. "To small steps that aren't really small at all."

They clinked their mugs together.

Kyle grinned. "Mine's going to sound silly in comparison, but... I'm setting a boundary around texting. No more answering Sidney's rapid-fire texts when I'm at work. I'm turning my phone off during meetings. She blows up my phone constantly, and it's driving me nuts."

Taryn smiled. "That's not silly at all. That's huge."

Kyle looked at her. "What about you?"

Taryn bit her lip. "I think... I'm going to tell Pete I'm not attending every church event with him. I need space. Time for *me*. I know he'll throw a fit, but... I have to try."

Kyle and Michelle both nodded with pride.

They sat in silence for a moment, letting the gravity of their small but mighty declarations settle.

Finally, Michelle spoke softly. "Do you guys ever wonder... what life could be like? If we really got out?"

Taryn swallowed hard. "All the time."

Kyle ran a hand through his hair. "It feels... impossible sometimes. But then we have nights like this, and I start to believe it could happen."

Michelle smiled, her eyes shining. "I hope so. I want... more. For me. For my kids."

Taryn looked at her friends, her heart swelling. "We're getting there. One step at a time."

And as they sipped their coffee and laughed over silly stories, something beautiful settled between them.

Hope. Real, fragile, stubborn hope.

And for the first time in a long time, that felt like enough.

Chapter 9

One Piece at a Time

Kyle sat in his car outside the group meeting, gripping the steering wheel so tightly his knuckles turned white. He hadn't moved for ten minutes. His heart thudded in his chest, and a deep, familiar shame crept up his spine.

Sidney had been in rare form that afternoon. She'd torn into him for being "emotionally unavailable," accused him of "never doing enough," and then stormed out, leaving a mess of slammed doors in her wake. All because he'd told her—gently—that he couldn't afford another last-minute weekend getaway.

Kyle exhaled shakily and finally stepped out of the car. He wasn't sure what he'd say tonight, but he needed... something.

Inside, the circle was already forming. Taryn smiled softly when he walked in, and Michelle patted the chair beside her.

"You okay?" Taryn whispered as he sat down.

He nodded, but his eyes told a different story.

Marilyn began. "Tonight's topic is *shame*. Narcissistic abuse often instills deep shame—making you feel that you're never good enough, that everything is your fault. I want to talk about how shame has shaped your sense of self, and what we can do to begin healing from it."

Kyle stared at the floor, his jaw clenched.

Gina started, her voice strong. "My ex used to tell me I was worthless every day. For years. Even after he left, I kept hearing those words in my head. I started to believe I *was* worthless."

Rachel nodded. "Me too. My boyfriend tells me no one else would ever want me. That I'm damaged goods. Sometimes... I think he's right."

Marilyn's voice was warm but firm. "You are not damaged goods. And their words—those lies—are not the truth."

Michelle spoke next, her eyes shining with tears. "Matt tells me... that I'm a bad mom. That I'm failing our kids because I'm not grateful enough. That... cuts the deepest."

Taryn nodded, her heart aching. "Pete tells me I'm a disappointment to God. That I'm a failure as a wife. And... after hearing it so many times, it's hard not to believe."

Marilyn looked around the room, her eyes full of empathy. "Shame keeps us small. It keeps us trapped. But you are all worthy of love, respect, and freedom. Their words say more about *them* than they ever will about you."

Then Kyle surprised everyone by speaking, his voice hoarse. "Sidney... she tells me I'm a loser. That I'm weak. And... the worst part? I agree with her. I *feel* weak. I don't know how to leave. I don't know if I can."

Silence fell over the group, heavy and raw.

Marilyn leaned forward. "Kyle... thank you for being honest. That's bravery. Weakness isn't staying. Weakness would be pretending this doesn't hurt you. What you did just now? That's *strength*."

Kyle's eyes filled, and he quickly swiped at them, embarrassed.

The meeting closed with quiet reflection. Marilyn handed out slips of paper with an affirmation: *"I am worthy. I am strong. I am enough."*

At The Corner Table

The trio sat in silence for the first few minutes after their coffee and pie arrived. Kyle stared down at his plate, pushing crumbs around with his fork.

Finally, Taryn spoke. "Kyle... I'm really proud of you tonight."

Michelle nodded. "Me too. That took a lot of courage."

Kyle let out a shaky breath. "It doesn't feel like courage. It feels... pathetic."

"It's not," Taryn said firmly. "You're breaking the silence. That's how it starts."

Michelle leaned in. "Do you... think about leaving?"

Kyle stared at his coffee. "Every day. But... every time I try to picture it, I freeze. She's all I've known for so long."

Taryn's heart ached. She saw so much of herself in his struggle. "It's okay to be scared. Change is terrifying. But... you're not alone."

Kyle looked up, his eyes red. "Do you guys ever feel like... no matter what we do, we're just going to end up back where we started?"

Michelle bit her lip. "Sometimes. But... I don't want to believe that's true."

They sat in silence, the clink of spoons and soft chatter around them filling the space.

Then Taryn spoke, her voice low. "You know what I've realized? Shame is their strongest weapon. If we can fight through that... even just a little... we start to take back pieces of ourselves."

Michelle smiled softly. "One piece at a time."

"One piece of pie at a time." Kyle joked.

Then he let out a breath and finally took a bite of pie. "Thanks, you guys. I don't say it enough, but... I'd be lost without you."

Taryn and Michelle exchanged a look, both of them tearing up.

Michelle reached across the table and grabbed his hand. "We're in this together."

Kyle squeezed her hand back, and Taryn joined in, their hands stacked in a quiet, powerful show of solidarity.

And in that moment, despite the heaviness, despite the shame still clinging to their hearts, they felt... stronger.

Together.

Chapter 10

Marilyn's Story

It was a rare quiet night at group. After a few moments of small talk, Marilyn leaned forward in her chair, her eyes scanning the room with warmth and gravity.

"I've been thinking," she began, "that it might be time I shared a little more about... me."

The group stilled. Taryn, Kyle, Michelle, and the others exchanged glances, surprised but curious. Marilyn always listened, always guided—but she rarely spoke about her own past.

She took a breath. "I know I sit here each week as your facilitator, but what you may not know is... I've sat exactly where you are."

Taryn's eyebrows lifted, and Kyle leaned in, his interest piqued.

"My first husband, Mark, was charming," Marilyn continued, her voice steady but threaded with memory. "The kind of man who could make anyone feel special. To the outside world, we were a golden couple—active in church, two beautiful kids, a lovely home. But behind closed doors, it was... another story entirely."

Her gaze softened, eyes far away as if watching old film reels of her life. "Mark was a master manipulator. It started small—criticisms disguised as jokes, subtle digs at my confidence. He had a way of making me feel like everything that went wrong was my fault. I convinced myself for years that if I just tried harder—if I prayed more, submitted more—things would change."

Michelle nodded slowly, eyes shining with understanding.

"But over time," Marilyn said, "the emotional abuse deepened. There were moments of pure cruelty. Nights when I sat up in bed, wondering how things had gotten so twisted. And yes—there were physical moments too. Times I told myself were accidents... until they weren't."

She paused, looking down at her folded hands. "It's strange, isn't it? How long we can endure, convincing ourselves we're being strong by staying."

Taryn felt her throat tighten, every word echoing her own experience.

Marilyn continued, her tone shifting to a quiet strength. "It took me 18 years to leave. Eighteen years of excuses, of shame, of spiritual guilt. I thought leaving would mean I'd failed God. That I wasn't being the 'godly wife' I was supposed to be."

She looked up, her eyes meeting each person in the circle. "But here's what I learned: God never called me—or any of us—to endure abuse. He calls us to life, to hope, to freedom. And when I finally left... yes, it was the hardest thing I've ever done. But it was also the beginning of my true healing."

She smiled gently. "I remarried years later—a good man, a kind man who shows me love in ways I didn't know were possible. But even before that, the real victory was reclaiming *myself*. Finding my worth again. And now? It's my deepest calling to walk beside others who are still finding their way."

Kyle wiped his eyes quietly. "I never knew, Marilyn."

Marilyn nodded. "I don't always share it. But I want you all to know... I'm not here just as a counselor. I'm here as someone who *gets it*. I've walked that road. And I know the power of community, of telling the truth, and of refusing to stay silent."

She handed out a new affirmation card, her hands steady. It read: *"My past shaped me, but it does not define me. I am worthy of love, safety, and respect."*

The group sat in stillness for a few moments, letting Marilyn's story soak in. There was something electric in the air—an unspoken bond, deeper now than ever before.

Taryn finally whispered, "Thank you. For trusting us with your story."

Marilyn smiled. "We heal in the telling. And we heal... together."

Chapter 11

Taryn's Knee Jerk Response

Taryn sat cross-legged on her living room floor, her journal open in her lap. The quiet hum of the ceiling fan was the only sound in the room. She was reflecting on what Marilyn had shared in group the night before. She had been writing steadily for over an hour, emptying her thoughts onto the page—grief, anger, small victories, and lingering doubts.

She paused, tapping the end of her pen against her knee.

Her knee.

It still ached, a dull, familiar throb that reminded her of everything she'd endured. Without meaning to, her mind drifted back—back to the moment that had marked a turning point in her story. The day her body bore the full weight of his rage. The day her own strength and defiance collided with the consequences she had always feared.

She closed her eyes, her hand resting on her scarred knee, and let the memory surface.

Taryn wasn't sure what the argument started over that day. By that point, most fights blurred together—spirals of accusation, gaslighting, and twisted words that felt designed to wear her down. But this one… this one was different.

This time, she stood her ground.

She was shaking, her heart pounding out of her chest, but she refused to back down. Pete had been on one of his tirades—

circling her like a vulture, spitting venom about how worthless she was, how lazy, how she was failing as a wife, as a mother, as a woman. And instead of shrinking, Taryn found herself rising. The words came tumbling out—decades of suppressed anger, grief, and exhaustion spilling into the space between them.

"No, Pete," she said, voice trembling but sure. "I'm done taking the blame. I'm done letting you twist everything. You're the one destroying this family."

Pete's eyes narrowed, his body tensing. Taryn had seen that look before. Cold. Empty. Dangerous.

She froze. Every instinct told her to step back, to de-escalate, to apologize for daring to speak up. But this time, she held her ground... until that familiar, terrifying flicker flashed across Pete's face.

The one she'd seen the night he threw her through a closed door so hard it broke the door jamb.

The one she'd seen when he hurled hot coffee at her face, and again when he whipped a coffee mug across the room, smashing it into her shoulder.

She knew that look. She knew what came next.

Suddenly, everything in her screamed: **Run.**

She bolted for the front door, her bare feet scrambling against the hardwood floor. She was so close—just steps away from the handle—when Pete's hand caught her from behind. With a force that stole her breath, he shoved her hard. Taryn's body slammed down onto the entryway tile, both knees taking the full brunt of the fall.

CRACK.

She heard it. Felt it. A sickening pop that echoed through her bones.

A cry tore from her throat, raw and guttural. Pain—unlike anything she'd ever felt—ripped through her legs, and she collapsed fully to the floor, clutching her knees. "Pete!" she screamed, gasping. "You really hurt me this time! I can't get up—oh my God—my knees—Pete, please, help me!"

But Pete stood there, silent, staring down at her. After a beat, he turned and walked away, disappearing into his office like nothing had happened. The door clicked shut.

Taryn lay there, sobbing, begging. Minutes passed. Ten… fifteen… twenty.

Finally, Pete emerged, wordless, and tossed a bag of frozen peas in her direction. The bag landed with a dull slap next to her crumpled body.

"Here," he said coldly. "Put this on the *'injury'* you inflicted on yourself."

And just like that, he was gone again.

The bruising came fast—deep, violent purples and swollen blue marks blooming across both knees. Taryn somehow dragged herself into the recliner and stayed there, ice pressed to her shattered knees, her body aching and her spirit broken. For days, she couldn't move without searing pain. Getting to the bathroom was an ordeal; standing, unbearable.

She wore shorts on purpose, not just because she was too swollen to wear pants, but she refused to cover the bruises. She wanted Pete to see. She wanted him to be confronted by the proof—**his proof.** But Pete wouldn't even look at her knees. He kept his distance, barricading himself in his office and muttering under his breath whenever she came near.

"She should be more careful," he said loudly to no one. "That's what happens when you act like a maniac. She's so clumsy. Honestly, she's lucky she didn't break her neck."

And when Taryn tried to bring it up—tried to hold him accountable, even just once—Pete responded the way he always did: with full-blown denial.

"That's not what happened, Taryn," he'd say, his voice dripping with false calm. "You fell. You lost your temper and tripped. I didn't even touch you."

And the worst part? He believed his own lies. Or at least, he convinced himself that they were true. He rewrote history with ease, turning himself into the victim every time.

Taryn sat alone most days that week, her knees throbbing, her soul hollowed out. She battled waves of guilt she couldn't fully explain. Guilt for what? For standing up to him? For speaking her truth? For getting hurt? It didn't make sense—but the shame clung to her like a second skin.

A doctor might have helped. But Taryn knew what would happen if she went to the ER. They would ask questions. They would document the bruises. They would *see* her.

And that was something Taryn wasn't ready to face—not yet.

So she sat. And iced. And prayed.

Weeks passed, but the bruises lingered. Even months later, her knees ached on cold mornings or after too much time on her feet. A year later, the pain still flared—sharp, insistent reminders of that day. The day her body broke... but her spirit *shifted*.

This injury wasn't like the others. It was a turning point. A wound too big to hide, too painful to ignore. Deep down, Taryn knew something had to change. She couldn't live like this forever.

And yet, Pete never relented. Even now, years later, he tells his version of the story, flipping it on its head.

"She's the abusive one," he says. "She's unstable. She's dangerous. That's the truth."

But Taryn knows the truth.
She always has.
And this time, she wouldn't let him rewrite it.

Chapter 12

Taryn's Breaking Point

The phone rang at 6:45 a.m.—jarring Taryn out of a restless sleep. She fumbled to grab it, heart racing, and saw Pete's name on the screen. He'd left early that morning to "pray and walk with God," as he often called his solitary outings.

She answered groggily. "Hello?"

"Where's my blue shirt?" Pete's voice was sharp, biting.

Taryn sat up, blinking. "Your blue shirt?"

"Yes, the *good* one. I have a meeting, and you didn't iron it."

Her stomach knotted. "Pete, it's in the closet. I ironed it on Tuesday."

He huffed, exasperated. "No. It's wrinkled. You know what? Never mind. Useless."

The line went dead.

Taryn stared at the phone, her hands shaking. How many times had mornings started like this? His contempt was like a poison she'd learned to swallow without flinching. But today, something was different. Something *snapped.*

She got up, dressed quickly, and grabbed her journal. She needed to write, to purge, to understand why her body felt like it was vibrating from the inside out.

Entry:

He called me useless again. Over a shirt. A stupid shirt. I feel like I can't breathe. Like my chest is closing in. Why do I let him keep doing this? Why do I stay?

Tears blurred the page. She pressed her pen down hard, carving the next words deep into the paper:

I deserve better. I know it. I just don't know how to leave.

Thursday Night Group

The group felt heavier that evening. Marilyn welcomed everyone with her usual warmth, but Taryn felt exposed, as if the weight of her morning phone call was stamped across her forehead.

Tonight's topic: *"The Power of No."*

Marilyn began, "Saying no is one of the simplest—and hardest—ways we set boundaries. For many of us, especially in abusive relationships, 'no' feels dangerous. But it's essential for healing."

Rachel spoke first. "I don't think I've said no to my boyfriend... ever. Not really. I'm scared of what would happen if I did."

Aaron nodded. "Same here. It's like... I know what'll happen: punishment. So it feels safer to just... give in."

Michelle's hands shook as she spoke. "Matt... he pushes and pushes. Even when I'm exhausted, when I say I can't... he keeps demanding. I've started practicing small nos. Like, 'No, I won't stay up late to wash your clothes.' It feels tiny, but... it's a start."

Kyle let out a slow breath. "Sid... if I say no to her, she goes nuclear. Threatens to leave. And honestly? That terrifies me. As messed up as it is... the idea of her leaving feels like failure."

Taryn's voice was quiet, but her eyes blazed. "Pete... he doesn't hear no. He *can't*. I've tried. Even on the smallest things. Like if I say no to going to a church event, or no to sex, or no to cleaning something immediately—it always turns into a fight. But... I'm starting to realize that not saying no hasn't protected me. It's just... erased me."

The group sat in solemn agreement.

Marilyn leaned forward. "Exactly, Taryn. Saying no is not just about them—it's about reclaiming *you*. Even if their response is ugly, your no matters. And over time, those nos build strength."

Marilyn ended the session with a mantra: *"I have the right to say no. My no is enough."*

At The Corner Table: The Weight of Expectations

That night, they stayed longer than usual. The pie was barely touched, their conversation heavier. The little corner table at the coffee shop had become their safe zone — a place where the weight of the group meetings could spill over into quiet conversation and laughter, far from judgmental eyes.

Tonight, though, the energy was heavier.

Michelle poked at her pie, her fork tracing circles in the whipped cream. "You know what's funny? I ran into an old coworker today. She said, 'Why don't you just leave, Michelle? You deserve better.'" She let out a sharp breath. "Like it's that simple."

Kyle nodded grimly. "Oh, yeah. Do you ever notice how people on the outside always want to tell you when you should leave?"

Taryn wrapped her hands around her mug, her shoulders tense. "They mean well... but they can never understand the process of leaving. It's not just packing a bag. It's peeling away years of shame, of fear, of everything tangled up inside you."

Michelle's voice softened. "Exactly. They don't see the work. The terror. The mental gymnastics. They just want to tell you when you should go — but they're not the ones doing the leaving."

Kyle added, "They're standing on the shore, yelling at you to swim faster, without realizing you're already exhausted just trying to stay afloat."

For a long moment, they all sat quietly, the hum of the coffee shop filling the space between them.

Taryn finally spoke, her voice low. "I'm glad I have you two. You're the only ones who actually get it."

Michelle reached across the table, squeezing Taryn's hand. "Same."

Kyle raised his coffee mug slightly. "Here's to doing it at our own pace. Not theirs."

"I've been thinking," Taryn said, stirring her tea absentmindedly. "About leaving."

Kyle and Michelle looked up quickly.

"I mean," she continued, "I've thought about it before. But now... I'm starting to *plan*. Quietly. Pete doesn't know. I'm looking at finances, housing... trying to figure out the logistics."

Michelle's eyes brimmed with tears. "Taryn... that's huge."

Kyle nodded. "And scary as hell. But... you can do it. You *deserve* to."

Taryn's voice wavered. "I'm terrified. But... something inside me is shifting. I can't keep living like this. Not forever."

They sat with her words, heavy and hopeful all at once.

Then Michelle surprised them. "I've been accepted for an interview."

Taryn gasped. "Michelle! That's amazing."

Michelle smiled through tears. "It's for the teaching job. Second grade. I don't know if I'll get it, but... it feels like a sign."

Kyle grinned. "You're both making moves. I feel like the slacker here."

Taryn shook her head. "You're doing the work too, Kyle. Every time you come here, every time you open up—you're moving forward."

Kyle looked down at his coffee, his voice low. "Thanks. That means a lot."

They raised their mugs again—an unspoken toast to small victories and the hope of something better.

Taryn's Night Alone

That night, Taryn sat at her kitchen table alone, the house eerily quiet. Pete was out—at a late-night prayer meeting, he'd said—but Taryn had her doubts.

She opened her journal and wrote:

I am scared. But I'm also strong. I said no today. No to ironing. No to pretending everything's okay. And tomorrow... I'll say no again. One step at a time.

She closed her journal, her chest rising and falling with deep, even breaths.

For the first time in a long time, she felt... alive.

Not just existing.

Alive.

Chapter 13

Rachel - The Good Girl

Rachel always showed up early. Hair in place, notebook neatly tucked in her lap, a soft smile for everyone who walked in. If someone needed a tissue, Rachel passed one. If Marilyn asked for a volunteer to read aloud, Rachel always raised her hand. The group saw her as the steady one. Reliable. Sweet. Strong.

But Rachel's story was a quiet kind of ache—the kind you couldn't see unless you listened closely.

She didn't cry much in group. Not like some of the others. Instead, she smiled while she spoke, even when her words cut deep.

"My husband doesn't yell," she said one night. "He doesn't hit. He just... sighs. Or leaves the room. Or makes me feel like I'm failing him without saying a word."

That night, after group, Rachel sat in her car for a long time. She didn't start the engine. Just stared out the windshield at the rain starting to gather in small rivers across the glass. She reached for her journal, flipped to a blank page, and wrote:

I am not crazy. I am not needy. I am not broken.

I just want to be loved without earning it.

She thought about the morning before group. How she had carefully laid out dinner for the evening, made sure the house was spotless, packed her husband's lunch, and kissed him goodbye. And still, when she said she was heading to therapy, he barely looked up from his phone.

"Oh. You're still doing that?"

She had nodded. Smiled. As if it didn't sting. As if she hadn't been rehearsing for days what she might say to the group that night.

She never told the others that she'd once spent an entire weekend in silence because he had said she "talked too much." Or that she had started hiding receipts for therapy payments because he'd told her it was a waste of money. Or that every time she brought up a boundary, he found a way to twist it into an accusation.

"You're supposed to be the Christian one," he'd say. "Where's the grace in walking away during a conversation?"

The conversations were never conversations. They were monologues with loaded pauses where she was expected to decode the right answer.

Rachel had grown up in church. Her mother taught Sunday School. Her father led worship. Her whole life, she had been the good girl. The peacekeeper. The one who colored inside the lines and never raised her voice.

She didn't recognize emotional abuse until Marilyn read the definition aloud in group.

"Abuse doesn't always come with bruises. Sometimes it comes as silence. As manipulation. As the steady erosion of your sense of self."

Rachel had stared at the floor that night, afraid to look up, afraid someone might see the truth finally sinking in.

It was Michelle who first spoke to her afterward. Not with advice or pity, but with simple presence.

"You don't have to keep proving your pain," Michelle said gently. "We believe you."

Rachel had gone home that night and cried. Really cried.

She was learning now that just because someone doesn't scream or shatter plates, it doesn't mean they aren't doing damage.

And slowly, painfully, Rachel was realizing: being the good girl wasn't saving her. It was silencing her.

That night, before bed, she opened her journal again and wrote:

I can be kind and still say no.
I can be patient and still ask for space.
I can be good and still deserve better.

Chapter Title 14

Aaron - The Apology Loop

Aaron always started his check-ins with an apology. "Sorry I'm late." "Sorry if I'm talking too much." "Sorry I didn't say more last week."

The group had started gently pushing back. Marilyn once smiled and said, "Aaron, what would it feel like to start with something besides 'sorry'?"

He had laughed nervously, eyes darting to the floor. "I guess... weird."

Aaron was in his late thirties, quiet but kind, the sort of man who made coffee for everyone before they even thought to ask. He was the kind of husband people called "dependable" — but what most didn't see was the constant fear that he might never be "enough."

He had married young. His wife, Jessa, was a whirlwind of charm and criticism. She ran the finances, managed the social calendar, and dictated the mood of the home. Aaron was always adjusting to her expectations, trying to avoid the edge of her anger. It wasn't screaming or slapping. It was ridicule. It was control.

"She tells me I embarrass her," he shared one night, eyes fixed on the floor. "She says I'm too soft. That I let people walk all over me... which is ironic, I guess."

The room had fallen still. Even Taryn had reached over and gently placed her hand on his.

Aaron had never said the word "abuse." Not until recently. He'd been conditioned to believe men couldn't be victims.

"I'm the guy. I'm supposed to be strong, right? How can I complain that she mocks me or controls the bank account? That she withholds affection for weeks because I forgot to take the trash out? It just sounds so... pathetic."

Marilyn looked at him softly. "Aaron, abuse doesn't have a gender. Pain is pain. Control is control."

He nodded slowly, as if letting those words settle into places they'd never been allowed to reach.

At home, Aaron lived in a cycle. Jessa would lash out or belittle him, and he would find a way to make it his fault. He would apologize. Buy flowers. Cook dinner. He had trained himself to soothe her storms before they fully landed. He called it love. But he was beginning to call it something else: survival.

One night after group, he sat alone in his truck, watching the steam rise off a cup of untouched coffee. He picked up his phone, opened a text to Jessa, then slowly put it down again. Instead, he opened his notes app and typed:

You don't have to stay sorry.
You don't have to shrink to be safe.
You don't have to carry it all to prove you're worth loving.

He didn't send the text. But he didn't delete it either.

That was enough for now.

Chapter 15

Michelle's Moment

Michelle stood outside the elementary school, clutching her worn leather purse tightly against her side. Her palms were sweaty, and her stomach fluttered with nerves. This was it—her first teaching interview in nearly six years. She glanced at her reflection in the glass door and gave herself a firm nod.

You belong here.

Walking through the halls brought back memories of the life she'd put on hold. The smell of pencil shavings, the brightly colored bulletin boards, the soft hum of children's laughter—it all felt achingly familiar, like visiting an old friend she didn't realize she'd missed.

The principal, a kind woman named Mrs. Delaney, greeted her warmly and led her to a cheerful office. They sat across from each other, and the questions began—about classroom management, lesson planning, and experience. Michelle felt rusty at first but soon found her rhythm, her passion for teaching shining through her nervousness.

When the interview wrapped up, Mrs. Delaney smiled. "You have wonderful experience, Michelle. We'll be in touch soon."

Michelle stepped back into the sunshine, her heart pounding with a mix of hope and fear. *No matter what happens,* she thought, *I did it. I showed up.*

Thursday Night Group

That evening, Michelle walked into the meeting room with an energy Taryn and Kyle hadn't seen in her before.

"You look... radiant," Taryn said, eyes wide.

Michelle blushed. "I had my interview today."

Kyle grinned. "No way! How'd it go?"

Michelle's smile was small but real. "I think... good. I don't know if I'll get the job, but just being there—it reminded me who I used to be. Before Matt. Before... all of this."

They hugged her tightly, sharing in her victory.

Marilyn called the group to order and introduced the night's topic: *"Gaslighting: The Art of Undermining Reality."*

"Gaslighting is when your abuser makes you doubt your own memories, perceptions, or sanity," Marilyn explained. "It's a powerful tactic to maintain control."

Rachel spoke first. "My boyfriend tells me I said things I *know* I didn't say. Or denies things he clearly did. I started keeping notes just to remind myself I'm not crazy."

Aaron nodded. "Same. My wife swears conversations never happened. It makes me feel... lost."

Kyle's voice was bitter. "Sid's a master at it. She'll twist things around so fast, I can't keep up. I leave conversations feeling like *I'm* the problem."

Michelle's smile faded. "Matt does it too. All the time. He tells me I'm imagining things, that I'm making stuff up to make him look bad. Sometimes I... wonder if he's right."

Taryn's eyes burned. "Pete... he tells me I overreact. That I 'misunderstand' him. When I bring up something hurtful he's done, he acts like I'm insane. I started to believe him."

Marilyn nodded. "Gaslighting is psychological warfare. It chips away at your confidence and your sense of self. But the fact that you *see* it—that's your power."

She handed out a new affirmation: *"I trust my memory. I trust my feelings. My truth matters."*

At The Corner Table

They sat, as always, in their booth with coffee and pie—blueberry this time.

"Do you ever just... get tired of feeling crazy?" Kyle asked, stirring his coffee slowly.

"All the time," Michelle said. "That's why today felt so good. Being at the school... I felt *sane* again. Like... I *know* who I am when I'm not constantly being questioned or torn down."

Taryn smiled warmly. "You should be so proud of yourself."

Michelle's eyes shone. "I am. For the first time in a long time... I really am."

Kyle leaned back. "What if we could all feel like that? Like... all the time?"

Taryn's face grew thoughtful. "I think... we're getting there. Slowly. Every time we say no. Every time we speak our truth. Every time we show up—for each other, and for ourselves."

Michelle lifted her mug. "To showing up."

They clinked mugs, their bond growing deeper, their hearts a little lighter.

Michelle's Quiet Night

That night, Michelle lay in bed, staring at the ceiling. Matt was snoring beside her, oblivious to the quiet victory unfolding inside her chest.

She whispered to herself, "I am worthy. I am strong. I am enough."

For the first time in a long time, she believed it.

Chapter 16

Kyle's Crossroads

Kyle stood in the aisle of a high-end boutique, staring blankly at a diamond bracelet shimmering under the glass. Sidney had texted him just an hour earlier: *"Saw this today. Would love it for our anniversary."*

Their anniversary was still two months away, but that never mattered to Sid. When she wanted something, she wanted it *now*.

Kyle's stomach churned. He knew the bracelet was out of his budget—way out—but the old, familiar script started playing in his head: *If I don't buy it, she'll be furious. She'll say I don't love her. She'll threaten to leave... again.*

He exhaled sharply, turning away from the counter. His heart raced as he walked out of the store without making a purchase.

One small step, he thought. *One boundary.*

But the guilt gnawed at him all the way home.

Thursday Night Group

Kyle arrived early, a rarity for him. Taryn and Michelle were already there, sipping tea and chatting quietly. He sat down heavily, rubbing his temples.

"You okay?" Taryn asked gently.

Kyle let out a bitter laugh. "Sid wanted a bracelet. Diamond. Expensive. I didn't buy it."

Michelle's eyes widened. "Kyle... that's amazing. I mean, hard, but... a huge boundary."

Kyle shook his head. "Yeah, but now she's blowing up my phone. Calling me selfish, cheap, heartless. Saying she deserves better."

Marilyn began the session just then, tonight's topic flashing on the whiteboard: *"The Trauma Bond: Why We Stay."*

"Trauma bonds," Marilyn explained, "are powerful emotional ties that develop through cycles of abuse and reward. You're hurt, then comforted. Dismissed, then adored. This push and pull creates a bond that's incredibly hard to break—even when you know it's toxic."

Rachel raised her hand. "That's *exactly* how it feels. Like... every time I think I'm ready to leave, he does something sweet, and I convince myself things will change."

Aaron added, "I feel addicted to those 'good' moments. Like they're crumbs of love I keep chasing."

Michelle spoke softly. "Matt... he can be cruel, but then he'll bring me flowers. Or tell me I'm beautiful. And I... cling to that."

Kyle's jaw clenched. "Sid does it too. I say no to something, she rages... but later she'll act like nothing happened. Be all sweet. It keeps me *hooked*."

Taryn's voice was low. "Pete's the same. It's like... just when I'm ready to give up, he becomes the man I *thought* I married. But it never lasts."

Marilyn nodded, her eyes kind. "Breaking a trauma bond takes time and support. You're not weak for staying. You're human. But the fact that you *see* the pattern means you're already breaking free—mentally and emotionally."

She handed out the week's affirmation: *"I deserve consistent love, not crumbs. I am breaking the cycle."*

At The Corner Table

The three sat together, each lost in their own thoughts.

"I hate how hooked I feel," Kyle admitted, stirring his coffee aimlessly. "Even when I *know* it's toxic, part of me still wants to fix it."

Michelle nodded. "Me too. It's like... we've been trained to accept so little, we start to believe it's all we deserve."

Taryn's eyes were sad but steady. "But we're learning. We're waking up. That's the difference."

Kyle sighed, leaning back. "I just wish I could fast-forward through the messy part."

They all laughed softly, knowing too well there was no fast-forward button for healing.

Michelle reached for her phone. "I keep reading articles about trauma bonds. About breaking patterns. I feel... hopeful. More than I've felt in a long time."

Taryn smiled. "Hope is everything."

They raised their mugs in another quiet toast, their friendship becoming the truest, healthiest bond in their lives.

Kyle's Night Alone

Back at his apartment, Kyle stared at his phone, seeing the angry texts piling up from Sidney.

He didn't answer.

Instead, he opened a blank note on his phone and typed:

Today I didn't buy the bracelet.
Today I set a boundary.
Today I chose me.

It wasn't everything. But it was a start.

And tonight, that was enough.

Chapter 17

Michelle Stands Strong

Michelle sat at the kitchen table, flipping through the mail when her phone buzzed. It was a text from Mrs. Delaney, the school principal: *"We'd love to offer you the second-grade teaching position! Please call me to confirm."*

Her breath caught in her throat. For a long moment, she just stared at the message, her heart pounding. After years of feeling trapped and small, here it was—a door swinging wide open.

"Mommy!" Kitty's tiny voice broke her trance. "Can you play blocks with me?"

Michelle blinked back tears, smiling as she knelt beside her daughter. "I'd love to, baby."

But her mind was spinning. She knew this job offer wasn't just a job—it was freedom. A way out.

Thursday Night Group

The energy in the room felt electric that evening. Marilyn announced the topic: *"The Cycle of Abuse: Why It's So Hard to Break Free."*

She drew a diagram on the board: tension-building, incident, reconciliation, calm. "This cycle repeats over and over," she explained. "And every time you think things are getting better, the cycle pulls you back in."

Aaron rubbed his temples. "It's scary how spot-on that is."

Rachel nodded. "I can tell you exactly where I am in that cycle any given week."

Kyle sighed. "Sid's in her calm phase right now. She's being sweet—texting me all the time, making dinner. But I know... it won't last."

Michelle looked at her hands, then raised her head. "Matt's been in the reconciliation phase. He's been complimenting me, acting... interested. But I see it now for what it is—a pattern. And I'm done."

Taryn's eyes widened. "What do you mean?"

Michelle took a deep breath. "I got the job. Full-time, second grade. I accepted it today."

Gasps of joy and congratulations filled the room.

Marilyn smiled warmly. "That's incredible, Michelle. You're reclaiming your independence—breaking the cycle."

Michelle's eyes glistened. "I'm terrified. But... I know it's the right step."

Marilyn handed out the week's affirmation: *"I am breaking the cycle. I am reclaiming my life."*

At The Corner Table

They sat in their usual spot, but tonight, the energy buzzed with excitement.

"I still can't believe it," Taryn said, grinning. "A full-time teaching job. Michelle, you're amazing."

Kyle smiled. "Seriously, you give me hope. If you can do it, maybe... someday I can too."

Michelle's eyes softened. "You *can,* Kyle. We all can. One step at a time."

Taryn leaned in, her voice thoughtful. "You know... we always said Michelle was the timid one. The quiet one. But look at her now."

Michelle blushed. "I never thought I had it in me. But... having you two in my corner—it changed everything."

They clinked their mugs, a celebration of growth, courage, and friendship—of family.

Michelle's Bold Move

Later that week, Michelle stood in the living room holding her letter of acceptance. Matt sat on the couch, staring at the TV.

She cleared her throat. "Matt, I took a full-time teaching job."

His head snapped up. "You *what?*"

"I'm going back to work. I start next month."

Matt's face twisted. "We *talked* about this. I told you—"

Michelle held up her hand, her voice steady. "I'm done talking. I'm doing what's best for me—and the kids."

For once, Matt was speechless.

And Michelle... felt powerful.

Chapter 18

The Shift

The morning sunlight streamed through Taryn's kitchen window as she sat alone, cradling her coffee cup between both hands. The house was unusually quiet—Pete had left early for a men's retreat, and the kids were still asleep upstairs. It was in these rare, peaceful moments that Taryn could hear her own thoughts clearly. And lately, those thoughts were getting louder.

Her journal lay open on the table. She stared at a sentence she'd written the night before: *"What if I actually leave?"* The words stared back at her, daring her to believe they were possible.

She traced the letters with her finger, heart thudding. It didn't feel like a fantasy anymore. It felt... like a plan starting to take shape.

Thursday Night Group

The room buzzed with quiet conversation as Marilyn set out handouts on the table. Tonight's topic was *"Future Faking and False Promises."*

Marilyn began, "Abusers often dangle a perfect future in front of you—promising change, love, commitment—only to keep you stuck in the same cycle. This is called future faking. It keeps you hopeful while nothing actually changes."

Rachel sighed. "My boyfriend always talks about 'someday.' Someday we'll get married. Someday we'll settle down. But... someday never comes."

Aaron nodded. "Same. My wife keeps saying things will be different after the next promotion. But it's been years, and nothing's different."

Michelle's face was tight. "Matt tells me he'll 'start appreciating me more' once the kids are older. But... I don't believe him anymore."

Kyle spoke bitterly. "Sid's classic line is, 'I'll stop when you stop pushing me.' Like it's my fault she cheats and lies."

Britney blurted out "My Mom says when I am older I will appreciate all that she does for me, but how do I appreciate someone who doesn't appreciate who I am right now?"

Marilyn turned to Taryn. "What about you?"

Taryn took a deep breath. "Pete's whole thing is spiritual promises. He tells me that if I just pray more, submit more, be more patient... then he'll change. Then God will bless us. But it's been *decades*. And nothing's different."

Marilyn's voice was calm but strong. "Future faking is one of the cruelest forms of manipulation because it feeds your deepest hopes. But real change isn't in promises—it's in consistent action. And if the action never comes, the promise is empty."

She handed out the week's affirmation: *"I deserve real love, not empty promises. I am worthy of true change."*

At The Corner Table

Tonight, the coffee shop buzzed with the usual hum of clinking cups and quiet chatter. But at their booth, the air felt different—more serious, more determined.

"I've been thinking about something," Taryn said, stirring her tea. "About how much time I've lost waiting for Pete to change."

Michelle nodded. "Me too. It's like... we keep holding on because of who we *hope* they'll become."

Kyle sighed. "Yeah. But we never get that version of them. Just... the same old cycle."

Taryn's eyes were bright, almost fierce. "I don't want to waste any more time. I'm done clinging to false promises."

Michelle reached across the table and squeezed her hand. "I'm so proud of you."

Kyle smiled. "Me too. You're leading the way for us."

Taryn shook her head. "We're all doing this. Together."

They raised their mugs once again, a silent vow to keep moving forward.

Michelle's Quiet Victory

Later that night, Michelle lay in bed beside Matt, staring at the ceiling. His snores filled the room, but her mind was racing. She thought about everything Marilyn had said—about future faking, about empty promises. And for the first time, she felt... clarity.

She whispered into the dark, "I'm done waiting."

Taryn's Alone Time

Back at home, Taryn stood in front of the bathroom mirror, studying her reflection. She didn't look all that different—same tired eyes, same worn lines around her mouth—but something inside her had shifted.

She whispered, "No more promises. No more pretending."

She smiled, just a little, and turned off the light.

Chapter 19

Four's a Crowd

Britney breezed into group that Thursday night with her usual upbeat energy, a bright scarf around her neck and her phone flashing with messages as she settled in next to Michelle.

"Hey, guys!" she chirped, her voice a little too loud for the quiet circle. "Oh my gosh, wait till you hear what happened this week."

Taryn and Kyle exchanged a quick look—the same look they'd been sharing more and more often lately. Exhaustion. Weariness. They had grown tired of Britney's constant one-upping, her tendency to mirror every story with her own slightly more dramatic version. It felt… performative, and while none of them wanted to be unkind, their patience had worn thin.

Marilyn began the session: "Tonight we're talking about gaslighting—how it erodes your trust in yourself."

Before anyone else could speak, Britney's hand shot up. "Oh wow, this is crazy," she began, eyes wide, "but my mom *literally* did that exact thing last night. She totally gaslighted me and said I imagined the whole argument we had. Like, I'm not dumb. I know what she said."

Taryn nodded politely, but her gaze drifted down to her lap. Kyle's jaw was tight, his foot tapping restlessly. Michelle just sat there, hands wrapped tightly around her coffee cup, listening but silent.

After the meeting, the three of them quietly gathered their things, hoping to sneak out unnoticed for their usual coffee ritual. But Britney was fast.

"Hey! Are you guys heading to the coffee shop?" she asked, smiling.

"Um, yeah," Taryn replied, hesitant. "Just a quick coffee."

"Great!" Britney beamed. "I'll tag along!"

At the diner, the mood was off. Britney chattered non-stop, asking question after question about what they usually talked about during their coffee meetups. Taryn and Kyle offered short, vague answers, sidestepping anything meaningful. The comfortable vulnerability they usually shared was gone, replaced by stiff, polite conversation.

After a long, awkward silence, Britney finally leaned back, eyes narrowing slightly.

"You guys are… really boring," she said bluntly. "I don't think I'll come back next time."

She grabbed her purse and stalked out.

For a moment, the three of them sat in stunned silence. Then Kyle let out a long breath and raised his hand for a high-five. "Mission accomplished," he said, grinning wryly. They all laughed a little too hard, relieved to have their safe space back.

But the laughter didn't last long.

The next week at group, Marilyn's face was tight, her voice softer than usual. "Before we begin tonight," she said, "I need to let you all know that Britney had a serious incident this week. She attempted to take her own life. Thankfully, she survived and is receiving care now. I know we all have different relationships in this room, but I want to remind you how fragile people can be, even when they seem okay on the outside."

Taryn felt her stomach twist into a hard knot. Michelle's eyes brimmed with tears almost instantly, her hand covering her mouth. Kyle stared down at the floor, unmoving, his knuckles white as he gripped his coffee cup.

No one spoke for a while. The weight of Marilyn's words sat heavy over them, pressing into their chests, filling the quiet with guilt and regret.

Later, as they sat at their corner table, the atmosphere was completely different. Gone was the light, relieved banter. Instead, they sat in silence, each lost in thought.

"I feel… awful," Michelle finally whispered, her voice trembling. "We weren't kind. We just… shut her out."

Kyle rubbed his hands over his face, eyes red. "We didn't *know*. We had no idea."

"But still…" Taryn said quietly, shaking her head. "We could have been gentler. More patient. She's just a kid. We don't know what battles people are fighting."

They sat in the quiet for a long time, the noise of the coffee shop swirling around them.

"I want to reach out to her," Michelle said at last. "We didn't handle things well. I don't want her to feel alone."

Taryn and Kyle both nodded, the unspoken agreement settling between them. Even as they fought their own battles, they were learning—sometimes the hard way—about grace, humility, and the messy, imperfect work of real friendship.

Chapter 20

The Unexpected Setback

Taryn's phone buzzed late in the evening. She was curled up on the couch, reading over apartment listings again—a nightly ritual lately. The message was from Pete: *"We need to talk when I get home."*

Her stomach dropped. She knew that tone all too well. She closed her laptop and took a deep breath, steadying herself for whatever storm was coming.

Pete came home an hour later, slamming the door behind him. "I talked to Brandon," he began, pacing the room. "He told me you've been... looking at apartments? Planning to *leave?*"

Taryn's face flushed hot. "Brandon shouldn't have—"

Pete cut her off, voice sharp. "I can't believe you'd do this. After *everything.* After all I've done for this family."

He began pacing, launching into a tirade of accusations—how she was ungrateful, how she was being swayed by Satan, how she was *destroying* the family. The words were all-too-familiar, but something inside Taryn felt... different this time.

She stood her ground, voice shaking but firm. "I'm done, Pete. Done with the manipulation. Done waiting for change that never comes."

Pete's eyes narrowed. "You'll regret this. We made a covenant before God. Taryn, you are possessed with an evil spirit. You need to be praying more."

She said nothing. But inside, she knew—this was her *line in the sand.*

Thursday Night Group

The group felt unusually quiet that evening. Taryn looked tired but determined.

Marilyn started the session: *"Tonight's topic: When You Hit the Wall—Recognizing Emotional Burnout."*

"Leaving an abusive situation takes enormous emotional energy," Marilyn said. "And often, we hit walls—burnout, fear, exhaustion—that make us question everything."

Kyle sighed. "I feel like I hit that wall every few weeks."

Rachel added, "I get so tired of fighting. Some days I just want to give up and pretend everything's fine."

Michelle, glowing a little brighter than usual, said quietly, "I think I'm finally past the wall. But it took... so long. And I still feel the fear creeping in."

Marilyn smiled gently. "That's normal. Courage isn't the absence of fear—it's action in spite of it."

Taryn finally spoke. "Pete found out. About my plans to leave. And... it was bad. But for the first time, I didn't crumble. I told him I was done."

Kyle's eyes widened. "Wow."

Michelle reached over and squeezed her hand. "You're incredible, Taryn."

Marilyn handed out this week's affirmation: *"Even when it's hard, I keep moving forward. My strength is greater than my fear."*

At The Corner Table

Tonight, the usual buzz of the coffee shop seemed distant as they sat together, heads close.

"You're so brave," Michelle said. "I don't know if I could have stayed that calm."

Taryn shook her head. "I wasn't calm. Inside I was shaking. But... I didn't back down."

Kyle leaned in. "What now?"

"I don't know," Taryn admitted. "But... I know I can't go back to *before.*"

They all sat in thoughtful silence for a moment before Kyle spoke up. "Funny, isn't it? How we thought you were the strongest one from the start. And now... it's like we're all taking turns being strong for each other."

Michelle smiled. "That's what friends do."

They clinked mugs again—quietly, reverently—feeling the weight of the journey they were all still walking.

Pete's Next Move

Later that week, Pete was on his best behavior—cooking dinner, complimenting Taryn, even bringing home flowers. But Taryn had seen the cycle too many times to be fooled. She watched quietly, eyes sharp, heart steeled.

This is just another phase, she reminded herself. *And I won't get pulled back in.*

Chapter 21

Kyle's Breaking Point

The Thursday group had just wrapped up, and Kyle lingered behind as Taryn and Michelle chatted near the door. His usual easy smile was missing tonight, replaced by something raw and unsettled.

"You okay?" Taryn asked gently.

Kyle hesitated. "I don't know. Something feels... different lately."

They sat down again, the room quiet except for Marilyn tidying her notes.

Kyle stared at his hands. "Sid and I had a huge fight last night. I caught her texting the guy I suspected she was seeing. Again. And when I confronted her..." he trailed off, shaking his head, voice thick with emotion, "she didn't even deny it this time. She just... smirked. Said it was my fault for not being enough."

Michelle let out a soft gasp. "Kyle... I'm so sorry."

He gave a hollow laugh. "The worst part? Even after that, I found myself *apologizing* to her. Like it was somehow my fault she cheated."

Marilyn sat down beside them, her tone calm but firm. "That's the cycle, Kyle. You've been conditioned to take the blame for her behavior. But her choices are hers alone."

Kyle's shoulders sagged. "I'm so tired of living like this. I keep saying I'm going to leave, but... I never do."

Taryn leaned in, her voice steady. "You're stronger than you think. You don't have to stay trapped."

There was a long pause, and then Kyle whispered, "I think... I'm finally done."

Michelle squeezed his hand. "We'll be here—every step of the way."

Kyle's Turning Point

The next few weeks were a blur of tension and quiet planning. Kyle moved his things into a small guest room at a friend's house. He filed paperwork. He blocked Sid's number more times than he could count—only to unblock it in moments of weakness, then re-block it after the inevitable guilt trips and manipulations.

In group, he shared the messy, complicated emotions: grief, guilt, anger, freedom—all tangled together.

"I thought leaving would feel like victory," he admitted one Thursday, eyes rimmed red. "But it mostly just feels... empty."

"That's normal," Marilyn reassured. "Ending a trauma bond is one of the hardest things you'll ever do. Your brain is wired to seek the familiar, even when it's toxic."

Michelle nodded. "I remember feeling the same when I started pulling away from Matt. You're detoxing, Kyle. Be gentle with yourself."

At The Corner Table

Sitting in their usual booth at the coffee shop, Kyle stared at his mug, silent.

Taryn broke the quiet. "You made the right call, Kyle."

"I know," he said after a beat. "It's just... weird. I keep thinking about the good times and wondering if I overreacted."

Michelle shook her head. "That's what keeps us stuck. You know the truth. Hold on to *that*."

Kyle looked at them, gratitude shining through his weariness. "I honestly don't know what I'd do without you two."

They clinked mugs, a silent promise to keep each other grounded.

Chapter 22

Too Fast, Too Soon?

The energy in group that Thursday night was noticeably different. Kyle bounded into the room with a grin so wide it practically lit up the place. He looked lighter—relieved, even—and both Taryn and Michelle exchanged curious glances.

"Kyle, you're glowing," Michelle teased as they settled in.

Kyle laughed, rubbing the back of his neck. "Well... I've got news." His eyes sparkled. "I met someone."

Taryn raised her eyebrows. "Already? Wow, that's... fast."

"I know, I know," Kyle said quickly, holding up his hands, "but it's different this time. Her name's Natalie. She's fun, easygoing... just—refreshing. We met through a friend at work, and we've been hanging out a lot."

Marilyn, overhearing, smiled warmly but didn't say much yet, letting the group dynamic play out.

Michelle leaned in, choosing her words carefully. "I mean, that's great, Kyle. You *deserve* to be happy. But... don't you think it's a little soon? You just left Sid not long ago."

Kyle nodded, his grin faltering slightly. "Yeah, I get that. But it's not like I'm jumping into anything super serious right away. I just... I don't know. I've been so alone, and Natalie's... she's kind of a breath of fresh air."

Taryn gave him a soft look. "We *get* it. Believe me. But you've worked so hard to start breaking those old patterns. Just... make sure you're not rushing back into something out of loneliness, okay?"

Kyle looked between them, visibly weighing their words. "Yeah," he said after a moment. "I appreciate you both saying that. Really. But this feels... good. Different."

Marilyn chimed in gently from her seat. "Sometimes things do feel different at first—especially after coming out of something painful. What matters is staying aware of the patterns and keeping an open dialogue with yourself—and with us."

Kyle nodded again, his grin returning. "I promise—I'll keep my eyes open. But for now? I'm just... enjoying it."

Michelle smiled warmly. "We're happy for you, Kyle. Truly. Just don't forget your worth along the way."

At The Corner Table

Later, the three sat at their usual booth, sipping their drinks.

"So," Michelle said with a playful smile, "tell us more about Natalie."

Kyle launched into stories about their dates—funny little details about her laugh, her love for old movies, how easy their conversations flowed. He sounded like a man *starved* for something light and joyful.

Taryn listened, smiling, but there was a flicker of worry in her eyes. When Kyle got up to refill his coffee, she turned to Michelle and whispered, "I really hope he's not falling too fast again."

Michelle sighed. "Me too. But all we can do is be here—and keep him grounded."

They clinked mugs, silent but united in their quiet resolve to watch out for their friend.

Chapter 23

Britney – The Mimic

Britney always arrived late and left early. She hugged her purse close to her chest like armor and spoke only when the silence stretched too long. Her stories shifted each week—details changed, timelines blurred. It made some people question her truth.

But Michelle saw something deeper: a girl desperate to belong.

At home, Britney was invisible unless she was in trouble. Her mother called her selfish, dramatic, and weak. If Britney cried, she was told to "stop playing the victim." If she stood up for herself, she was told she was ungrateful.

In group, Britney started to mimic the pain she heard—retelling it like it was her own. Not out of malice or deceit, but from a hollow ache to be understood.

"I know I'm probably annoying," she mumbled one night, her voice barely above a whisper. "I just… I don't know what's real anymore."

Marilyn responded gently. "When we've spent a long time being silenced, our voice can feel foreign. You're not annoying. You're searching. That takes courage."

That night, Britney sat in her room with a journal open, chewing on the cap of her pen. She had written and scribbled out the first sentence a dozen times. Finally, she settled on:

Today, I spoke. They didn't laugh. They didn't leave. They listened.

The next Thursday, Britney arrived early for the first time. She brought muffins and a shy smile. Taryn nodded to her, Michelle scooted over to make room, and Kyle passed her a napkin without saying a word.

After group, they all lingered in the parking lot, talking and laughing. Britney stood to the side, unsure whether to join. Michelle caught her eye.

"Corner table?" she asked.

Britney's face lit up. "Really? You sure?"

"Come on," Taryn added, holding the door. "We've got a spot just for you."

It was the first time Britney felt like part of something real.

Later that night, alone in her room, she journaled again:

Today, I belonged.

Chapter 24

Gina: The Door That Closed

Gina rarely spoke in group. She sat near the back, arms crossed, expression unreadable. Her eyes flicked around the room, sharp and quiet, like she was collecting information but never giving anything away.

She always said she was just there to listen. But one night, after everyone had shared, Marilyn gently asked, "Gina, would you like to speak tonight?"

Gina hesitated. Then, in a voice low but steady, she said, "I don't even know where to start. I guess... I'm still trying to figure out if what I went through counts."

No one interrupted. No one rushed her.

There was a heaviness in the air before Gina even spoke. Maybe it was the way she clutched the sleeve of her cardigan, fingers twisting the fabric like she was unraveling a thread only she could see.

"I wasn't going to share tonight," she said softly, "but... something's been stirring."

The circle waited. No one rushed her. Gina wasn't the type to perform her pain. She'd spent too long surviving in silence to waste words now.

"I think about that night sometimes. The door. Him standing on the other side of it. I used to dream about that moment—the knock, the apology, the confession that he couldn't live without me. I waited months for that knock. But it didn't come the way I imagined."

Her voice didn't shake. It sharpened.

"It was Christmastime. Cold. I was in pajamas, still clinging to hope like it was a virtue. Carl had been stringing me along for months. He told me, 'Just one more month. Let me figure things out with Kelly. Then I'll come back to you.' And I believed him. Every time."

Gina didn't look at anyone. She stared past the group, like the story still lived behind her eyes.

"But that night, when he finally showed up... Kelly was with him."

A murmur rippled around the circle.

"They were dressed up, all smiles and glitter, just back from the company Christmas party—the one he used to take me to. He knocked like it was nothing. And when I opened the door, he said, 'Gina, This is the woman I love. She does not believe that I am through with you. I am through with you. You need to accept that.'" Carl looked so pleased with himself, like he had just won a prize or something.

She paused. "Except he wasn't asking. He was declaring. Like my heart was a courtroom, and he was delivering the final verdict."

Someone whispered, "God..."

Gina smiled, bitter and distant. "And the wild part? I let them in."

She exhaled, almost laughing at herself.

"Maybe it was shock. Or maybe it was codependency—I didn't know how to value myself enough to slam the door shut. We sat. We talked. I told Kelly that Carl had promised—if I just gave him one more month, he'd leave her. She froze. Then she said, 'He told me the same thing.'"

Gasps now. Quiet curses.

Gina's voice dropped.

"I told her about the miscarriage. I was in the hospital, bleeding, broken, and Carl didn't come. He said he had to take her waterskiing."

She paused to swallow the memory.

"Kelly looked at him and said, 'You mean it was your child?' And I looked at him and said, 'You told her it wasn't.'"

Silence. Thick and aching.

"That was the moment we both realized—he had lied to us both. And they showed up thinking they were some kind of couple with closure, but it backfired. She saw it. Finally. And I… I started to."

Gina wrapped her arms around herself. "But I still didn't walk away. Not right then. I stayed."

Her voice wavered now. Raw.

"A few months later, I got pregnant again. And that's when Carl changed. Not just the lies—not just the manipulation. It got darker. More violent. He didn't hit me. He didn't have to. His words were weapons."

She looked down at her hands.

"When I told him, he went silent. Then cold. And then… he threatened me."

No one moved. No one breathed.

"He told me that if I didn't get an abortion, he would kill himself. He said he'd come to my apartment, walk into my bedroom, and blow his brains out. He said it would be my fault—that I'd be the one who would have to find him. That I would have to live with what I'd done to him. That I was selfish for getting pregnant."

There were quiet tears around the room. Not from Gina. She had already cried those tears.

"I lived in fear. Not just of losing him—but of what he might do. Of waking up to that. Of having blood on my hands that wasn't mine. And for weeks, I felt trapped—like I was carrying a ticking bomb inside me, and it was all my fault."

She swallowed.

"I don't want to talk about what I chose. Not tonight. That part still hurts. But I will say this—**that wasn't love**. That was abuse. Psychological warfare disguised as intimacy. A man who would rather make me responsible for his life—or his death—than take ownership of his own choices."

Her voice steadied again.

"It took Marilyn—my therapist—two years to help me untangle all the ways I thought that kind of suffering was proof of devotion. I used to say, 'If I stay, maybe I can love him into healing.' But she said, 'If you stay, you'll lose the pieces of yourself you're trying to save.'"

Gina blinked hard. "She was right."

"I haven't seen Carl in years. Last I heard, he's still living with his mom. He's nearly forty. That used to make me feel sad. Now? It makes me feel free."

She looked up.

"I come to group because I want to remember how far I've come. Because I see women in this circle who are where I once was. And when I see them choosing themselves... it reminds me that I did, too."

Someone across the room reached for her hand. Another gently nodded through silent tears.

"And I'll never forget what Marilyn told me in one of our last sessions: 'You are not hard to love. You were just trying to be loved by someone who didn't know what love was.'"

The room held its breath.

Gina offered a small, quiet smile. "And I don't need to keep my door open anymore. Not for him. Not for anyone who can't walk through it with respect."

Because sometimes healing isn't loud—it's the quiet knowing that the door you closed saved your life.

Chapter 25

A Taste of Freedom

The apartment key turned in the lock with a satisfying click. Taryn stepped inside, holding her breath. It was empty, echoey, and smelled faintly of fresh paint—but to her, it was *sanctuary*.

She dropped her purse on the kitchen counter and slowly walked through each room, taking it all in. The second bedroom was barely big enough for a bunk beds and a dresser, but Kenny and Kate were thrilled and excited to share their new room. The carpet had seen better days, and the linoleum in the kitchen was peeling at the corners. But none of that mattered. Every square foot whispered: *Freedom*.

She stood by the window, sunlight streaming through half-bent blinds, and let her shoulders sag. After years of walking on eggshells, this space was quiet. Peaceful. And completely hers.

Her phone buzzed in her pocket—a text from Brandon.

Brandon: *Mom, I'm so proud of you. Wish I could be there to help unpack.*

She hesitated, her finger hovering over Brandon's name in her contacts. They hadn't spoken much since the blowup with Pete. This was Brandon's way of apologizing—of breaking the ice.

Taryn smiled, tears stinging her eyes. She tapped out a reply:

Taryn: *Thank you, honey. Love you so much.*

Just then, there was a knock at the door—Michelle along with her kids, and Kyle, each balancing coffee trays and bags of breakfast sandwiches.

"Mommy" Kate said, "Can Kitty and Kevin come play in our new room?"

"Of course" Taryn, responded with a bit of glee in her voice.

"Their new room." She beamed at Kyle and Michelle.

"Let's DO this!" Kyle said, stepping inside and spinning dramatically in the tiny living room. "Welcome home, Taryn."

Michelle hugged her tight. "It's perfect. Absolutely perfect."

Taryn laughed through fresh tears. "Thank you guys... really. I don't think I could do this without you."

They unloaded boxes from their cars—plates, books, pillows, knick-knacks—and made it their mission to set up as much as possible in one day. They cranked up a playlist of cheesy '90s pop hits, singing off-key as they worked. Kyle tackled the bookshelf, grumbling over missing screws; Michelle folded Taryn's kitchen towels with precision; Taryn herself scrubbed the bathroom until it gleamed.

Around noon, they took a break, flopping onto the floor with pizza and sodas. The air buzzed with exhaustion—but also with joy.

"So what's the first thing you're going to do tonight?" Michelle asked, biting into her slice.

Taryn smiled, thinking. "I don't know... maybe light a candle and just... sit. In the quiet. No lectures. No lists. No one telling me how I'm failing."

Kyle nodded, looking serious. "You deserve that. All of it."

For a moment, they sat in comfortable silence, watching sunlight filter through the window. It was such a simple thing, and yet... monumental.

"Honestly?" Taryn added softly, "I don't even know who I am without Pete telling me who I am. But... I'm excited to find out."

Michelle raised her soda can high. "To new beginnings."

They clinked cans, laughter bubbling up like relief.

That Night

After the last box was unpacked and her friends had left with tight hugs and promises to check in soon, Taryn stood alone in the middle of her new home. She turned in a slow circle, taking it all in—the quiet hum of the fridge, the faint scent of new sheets, the calming emptiness.

She opened a drawer and found an old scented candle she'd forgotten about—vanilla and sandalwood—and lit it on the coffee table. The glow flickered, warm and soft, like hope itself.

After the kids giggled themselves to sleep, she curled up on the couch, pulling a blanket around her shoulders. At first, the silence was deafening. No heavy footsteps. No muttered insults. No creak of the bedroom door slamming.

And for the first time in a long time, she breathed deeply, fully, without fear of what might happen next.

Her phone buzzed—a message from Pete.

Pete: *I hope you're proud of yourself. Destroying our family. Hope your new place is worth it.*

Taryn stared at the screen for a long moment. The old Taryn would have crumbled, desperate to explain herself, to smooth things over. But this Taryn... she locked her phone and set it face down on the table.

She whispered into the quiet, "Not tonight, Pete. Not anymore."

Lying in bed later, the loneliness crept in—but so did something else: peace. A fragile, flickering peace, but peace nonetheless.

Her final thought before falling asleep was simple and powerful:

I am free.

Chapter 26

Breaking Old Habits

Kyle sat on the couch, nervously tapping his foot. Across from him, Natalie—his new girlfriend—laughed loudly at something on her phone, completely ignoring him. He'd been dating her for a few months now, and at first, it had felt like everything Sid wasn't: fun, fresh, flirty.

But cracks were starting to show.

"I thought we were going to talk about the trip," Kyle ventured.

Natalie didn't look up. "Hmm? Oh, yeah. You can just book it. Whatever's easiest."

Kyle frowned. He'd already paid for the last two trips, plus the gifts and dinners, and now she was dropping hints about a new purse she wanted. A familiar pit formed in his stomach.

Not again, he thought. *Please don't let this be happening again.*

Thursday Night Group

Kyle walked into group looking distracted. Taryn and Michelle exchanged a glance but said nothing at first.

Marilyn introduced tonight's theme: *"Recognizing New Patterns: Avoiding the Same Trap."*

She began, "It's common to break free from one toxic relationship only to find yourself in another—often without realizing it at first. This is because unresolved patterns can draw us back to familiar dynamics."

Rachel raised her hand. "It's scary. Like... I thought I'd learned my lesson, but I keep picking the same kind of guy."

Aaron nodded. "Me too. Different face, same dysfunction."

Marilyn turned to Kyle. "Kyle, you've been quiet tonight."

Kyle hesitated, then sighed. "I think... I'm doing it again. My new girlfriend, Natalie... she seemed amazing at first. But now... she's starting to feel a lot like Sid."

Michelle's eyes were full of sympathy. "What's been happening?"

Kyle rubbed his temples. "She's... using me. For money. For trips. For attention. And I keep *letting* her."

Marilyn's voice was gentle. "Awareness is a huge step. Recognizing the pattern is the first key to breaking it."

Taryn chimed in. "Kyle... don't beat yourself up. It's so easy to slip back into familiar roles. But you *see* it now. That's growth."

Kyle nodded, eyes damp. "It just... hurts. I wanted this one to be different."

Marilyn handed out the week's affirmation: *"I am worthy of healthy, mutual love. I will not settle for less."*

At The Corner Table

Kyle sat with his head in his hands. "I feel like an idiot," he muttered.

Michelle put a hand on his arm. "You are *not* an idiot. You're human. You want love. That's not a crime."

Taryn added softly, "And now that you see it... you get to *choose* differently."

Kyle gave a half-hearted smile. "I know. I just... wanted to believe so badly."

They sat in comfortable silence for a while, each lost in thought.

Then Michelle said, "You know what I realized? We've all had blind spots. But we're not blind forever. We learn. We grow."

Kyle smiled a little wider. "Here's hoping."

They clinked mugs, silently vowing to keep showing up for each other—no matter how messy the road got.

Kyle's Moment of Truth

Later that week, Kyle sat across from Natalie at a trendy café. She was scrolling through her phone again, barely looking at him.

He took a deep breath. "Natalie... I think we need to talk."

She looked up, eyebrows raised. "Uh-oh. That's never good."

He pushed forward, heart pounding. "I feel like... I'm not getting what I need in this relationship. And honestly... I think it's time we part ways."

Natalie stared at him, stunned. "Are you *serious?* After everything I've *put up with* from you?"

Kyle blinked, momentarily thrown by the twist. But then he smiled—a real, calm smile. "Yeah. I'm serious."

And for the first time in a long time, he felt... free.

Chapter 27

More of the Same

The house was quiet except for the faint hum of the dishwasher. Taryn stood in the hallway, clutching her phone tightly. Pete had just sent a text: *"Doctor says it's cancer. I don't have long."*

She sat down hard on the stairs, her heart pounding. After everything—after finally building her courage, after standing up to him—this.

Her first reaction was disbelief. Then confusion. And then... guilt.

What if he really is dying?
What if this is my last chance to do the right thing?
What if I'm a terrible person if I don't stay?

The swirl of questions was suffocating. Deep down, she knew Pete's patterns too well to trust anything at face value. But the fear... the guilt... it was *stronger* than her doubts.

She put her head in her hands, tears pricking her eyes. This wasn't the way it was supposed to happen.

Thursday Night Group

That week, Taryn looked hollowed out, her usual spark dimmed. Kyle and Michelle exchanged worried glances as they sat down.

Marilyn opened the session with tonight's topic: *"Guilt: The Abuser's Favorite Weapon."*

"Guilt," Marilyn said, "is often used to keep us tethered to unhealthy situations. Whether it's guilt about leaving, guilt about children, or guilt over 'breaking' a family—it's powerful. But guilt doesn't mean you're wrong. It means you're human."

Aaron spoke up. "My wife tells me every time I mention leaving, I'm ruining our kids' lives. It kills me."

Rachel nodded. "My boyfriend says he'd fall apart without me. I feel responsible for his happiness."

Britney spoke up with an unusually soft tone, "My Mom, she...she said that my suicide attempt was to hurt her. Her...she thinks my wanting to die was to hurt *her*."

They were all shocked.

The room fell silent.

Michelle squeezed Britney's hand and said. "We are here for you Britney, you are not alone."

Michelle glanced at Taryn, concern in her eyes. "Matt does the same. He always plays the victim when I get stronger."

Marilyn looked gently at Taryn. "You're quiet tonight."

Taryn swallowed hard. "Pete... says he has cancer. He wants me to come home."

The room fell silent again.

Michelle finally spoke. "Do you believe him?"

"I don't know," Taryn whispered. "Part of me... wants to believe. But another part... knows his games."

Marilyn leaned forward. "It's okay to feel conflicted. But remember—no one gets to *own* your life. Not even in sickness."

She handed out the week's affirmation: *"My worth is not defined by guilt. I choose what's best for me."*

At The Corner Table

The coffee shop felt heavy that night. Taryn stirred her tea absentmindedly, staring into the cup.

"You don't owe him your life," Michelle said softly.

Taryn sighed. "But what if he *is* dying? What if I walk away and regret it forever?"

Kyle shook his head. "Taryn... you've given him *everything*. You don't owe him your *soul*."

Taryn blinked back tears. "It just feels... impossible."

Michelle reached across the table. "Whatever you decide, we're with you."

Kyle added, "No judgment. Ever."

They clinked mugs—this time without words—each of them feeling the weight of Taryn's impossible choice.

Taryn's Decision

A week later, Taryn and the kids stood at Pete's front door, suitcases in hand. He opened the door with a practiced look of weariness, arms open as if he were already the tragic hero.

She stepped inside, her heart breaking into quiet pieces. She was only here for the weekend; she kept telling herself. This is not my home anymore.

I stayed. I endured. Until I barely existed.

And she knew, deep down, she was stepping right back into the same storm.

Chapter 28

Michelle Extends an Olive Branch

Michelle stood at the front of her second-grade classroom, smoothing the edges of a colorful bulletin board. Bright letters spelled out: *"Welcome to Our Year of Learning!"* Kitty and Kevin had helped her pick out the decorations, and their tiny handprints were hidden in the corner of the wall art—her little secret reminder of why she was doing all this.

The bell rang, and twenty eager faces filed in. As she guided them to their desks, a quiet pride bloomed inside her chest. This—this was *hers*. A space where her voice mattered, where she was in control, where she was safe.

Thursday Night Group

Michelle was beaming when she arrived. Even Taryn, still raw and quiet, gave a small smile.

Marilyn introduced the evening's topic: *"Thriving, Not Just Surviving."*

"So many of us get stuck in survival mode," she explained. "But real healing means learning to thrive—to dream, to build, to *live fully* again."

Aaron said, "Honestly, I don't even know what thriving *looks* like."

Rachel added, "Me either. It's been survival for so long."

Marilyn smiled. "Thriving starts small. One brave decision at a time."

Britney added, "One brave decision at a time. I am ready to start being brave."

Michelle raised her hand. "I started my new job last week. It's... hard, and exhausting, but for the first time in years, I feel *alive*."

Applause broke out around the room.

Taryn's voice was soft but sincere. "I'm so proud of you, Michelle."

Michelle's eyes glistened. "Thank you. I didn't think I could ever get here. But... step by step, I did."

Marilyn handed out the week's affirmation: *"I am not just surviving. I am building a new, beautiful life."*

At The Corner Table

Michelle sat at the corner table, stirring her tea absentmindedly. Taryn and Kyle exchanged a glance—something was different about her tonight. Not just the new job glow... something else.

Finally, Taryn asked gently, "You okay? You've been quiet."

Michelle let out a breath she'd been holding. "It's... done. Really done."

"What do you mean?" Kyle asked, leaning forward.

Michelle's eyes shimmered with unshed tears—but this time, they weren't just sadness. They were relief. "Matt moved out today. He's gone."

Taryn's hand flew to her mouth. "Oh, Michelle."

"I told him last week," Michelle said, her voice trembling but sure. "I told him I couldn't live like this anymore. That I deserved better—and so did the kids. At first, he laughed. Said I'd never make it on my own. But when he saw I wasn't backing down... he packed a bag and left."

Kyle's eyes widened. "Wow. How are you feeling?"

Michelle wiped at her eyes. "Honestly? Terrified. But free. And for the first time in so long... hopeful."

Taryn squeezed her hand. "You are so brave."

Kyle lifted his mug. "To fresh starts."

They all clinked their drinks together, the air humming with something new: **victory.**

The energy was lighter than it had been in weeks. Kyle and Taryn listened as Michelle shared stories about her students—the funny things they said, the drawings they gave her.

"It's like... they see me," Michelle said, eyes shining. "And they don't expect anything from me except kindness."

Kyle grinned. "I'm telling you, you're a natural."

Taryn added, "You deserve every bit of this happiness."

Michelle hesitated, then said, "I've been thinking about Britney. I know we... didn't handle things well before. But maybe it's time to reach out. To offer real support."

Kyle nodded. "I think that's a beautiful idea."

Taryn smiled. "She could really use someone like you."

Michelle felt a wave of peace. "I think... I'm ready to be that person."

Michelle's Full Circle Moment

That weekend, Michelle texted Britney, inviting her for coffee. Britney responded almost immediately: *"I'd love that. Thank you."*

They met at the coffee shop where so many of Michelle's own healing conversations had taken place. Britney looked nervous, but her eyes lit up when Michelle hugged her warmly.

They sat and talked for hours—no judgment, no competition, just two women sharing their stories, their pain, their hope.

As they left, Britney whispered, "I didn't know people could be this kind."

Michelle smiled. "You deserve kindness. And you're not alone anymore."

Chapter 29

Alone Again, and it's Okay

Kyle sat alone in his apartment, staring at the emptiness around him. Natalie was gone now, her absence both a relief and a deep ache. He had broken free, yes—but the silence left behind was deafening.

His phone buzzed. A text from Taryn: *"How are you holding up?"*

Kyle hesitated, then typed back: *"Lonely. But okay."*

Moments later, another text came through: Michelle. *"Proud of you. Stay strong. Coffee soon?"*

He smiled faintly, grateful for the net of support holding him up.

Thursday Night Group

Tonight's session was different. Marilyn dimmed the lights and placed a single candle in the center of the table.

"Our topic tonight," she said gently, "is *Emptiness After Breaking Free*. We don't talk about it enough—but leaving a toxic relationship often feels lonelier than we expect. We've been so entangled that the absence feels like grief, even when it's a good thing."

Rachel whispered, "It's like losing a part of yourself."

Aaron nodded. "I thought leaving would make me instantly happy. But... I just feel lost."

Marilyn smiled softly. "That's normal. Healing is messy. We grieve not just the person, but the *dream* we held onto for so long."

She looked at Kyle. "Do you want to share?"

Kyle's voice was low but clear. "I thought ending things with Sid, and then Natalie would feel... victorious. And it *does,* in a way. But mostly, I just feel... empty. Like I don't know who I am without someone to pour my energy into."

Michelle reached over, squeezing his hand. "It'll get better, Kyle. You're finding *you* now."

Marilyn handed out this week's affirmation: *"I am whole, even when alone. My healing belongs to me."*

At The Corner Table

"I don't know how to *be* single," Kyle admitted, staring into his coffee. "I've always jumped from one relationship to the next."

Michelle nodded. "It's scary at first. But... it's also freeing. You get to figure out what *you* want. What *you* need."

Taryn added quietly, "And you have us. You're not alone."

Kyle smiled, gratitude shining in his eyes. "You guys... you've saved me more than you know."

They lifted their mugs again—a silent toast to the bravery of rebuilding.

Kyle's Quiet Victory

A few days later, Kyle sat at home, a new journal in his lap. He began to write:

"Today, I choose me. I choose healing. I choose wholeness. For the first time in my life, I'm learning to love myself without needing someone else to fill the gaps. It's scary. But it's mine."

He closed the journal, a small smile tugging at his lips. For the first time in a long time, he felt... hopeful.

Chapter 30

The Guilt Trip

It was a rainy Thursday when Taryn's phone buzzed—a message from Pete: *"Starting my chemo next week. Could use your support. I'm scared."*

She sat frozen, the storm outside mirroring the one inside her chest. Every instinct screamed to stay away, but guilt wrapped around her heart like a vice. Her friends' words echoed in her head: *You don't owe him your soul. Stay strong.*

But it was hard. So hard.

Later that evening, Taryn found herself in her car, engine running, staring at Pete's street from a distance. She didn't get out. But she also didn't drive away.

Thursday Night Group

Marilyn opened the session with tonight's topic: *"Compassion vs. Codependency: Knowing the Difference."*

She drew two columns on the whiteboard.
Compassion: empathy, healthy boundaries, shared responsibility.
Codependency: over-functioning, rescuing, loss of self.

"Compassion says, 'I care *with* you.' Codependency says, 'I'll carry it *for* you.'"

Aaron asked, "But how do you *know* which one you're doing?"

Marilyn smiled. "Good question. Ask yourself: Am I neglecting my own needs? Am I the only one working to fix things? Am I acting out of guilt or fear? Those are red flags."

Taryn sat quietly, her face pale.

Michelle turned gently toward her. "Do you want to share?"

Taryn's eyes filled with tears. "Pete's starting chemo. He texted me... said he was scared. I... I went to his street today. I didn't knock. But... I *wanted* to."

Silence fell, heavy and understanding.

Kyle finally said, "Taryn, that's... so hard. But remember... he *always* pulls you back when you're about to break free."

Taryn nodded, wiping her eyes. "I know. I just... I feel cruel. Like... what if this time he *really* needs me?"

Marilyn's voice was steady. "It's not cruel to protect yourself. Compassion includes *you, too.*"

The affirmation that week felt deeply personal: *"I can care, but I cannot carry. I deserve peace, too."*

At The Corner Table

Taryn stirred her tea, lost in thought.

Michelle said softly, "You don't have to decide today. But... be honest with yourself about what you can handle."

Kyle added, "And whatever happens... we've got you."

Taryn smiled weakly. "You guys are my anchor. Thank you."

They clinked mugs—this time in quiet solidarity—holding space for the impossible choice Taryn faced.

Taryn's Choice

That weekend, Taryn sat on her bed, Bible open on her lap. Tears fell freely as she prayed aloud.

"God... I don't know what to do. I want to help, but I don't want to lose myself again. Please... give me wisdom."

Her phone buzzed. Pete again. *"I miss you. I'm sorry for everything. Please come home. I need you."*

Her heart clenched.

She closed her eyes, whispering, "Help me let go... or help me survive if I can't."

And in that quiet room, Taryn realized: no matter what she chose, this was her cross to bear—and hers alone.

Chapter 31

Britney's Breakthrough

Michelle sat across from Britney at their usual corner table, watching her stir her coffee nervously. It had been a few weeks since Michelle first reached out, and little by little, Britney had opened up more.

Today, Britney looked different—tired but determined.

"I need to tell you something," Britney said, her voice low. "I... I tried to talk to my mom. I told her I needed space. And... she flipped out. Called me ungrateful. Told me I was ruining her life."

Michelle's heart ached, but she kept her tone calm. "I'm so sorry, Britney. That's really hard. How did you respond?"

Britney bit her lip. "I almost apologized like I always do. But... I didn't. I told her I love her, but I *meant* what I said."

Michelle's eyes lit up. "Britney, that's huge. That's *boundaries*."

Britney blinked back tears. "It felt awful. But also... kind of freeing?"

Michelle smiled. "Exactly. It *will* feel uncomfortable at first. But you're starting to stand up for yourself."

Britney's voice trembled. "I don't want to end up like... trapped. Like..."

She trailed off, but Michelle understood. Like Taryn. Like so many others.

Michelle reached across the table. "You won't. You're already changing your story."

Thursday Night Group

The room felt different that night—almost electric. Marilyn began, "Tonight's topic: *Celebrating Small Wins.* It's easy to focus on what's still broken, but we also need to recognize how far we've come."

Rachel spoke up. "I finally told my boyfriend no... and I stuck to it."

Aaron added, "I didn't answer my wife's 15th angry text today. That's a win for me."

Britney raised her hand shyly. "I set a boundary with my mom. It... wasn't easy. But I did it."

The group clapped and smiled warmly at her.

Michelle squeezed her hand. "So proud of you."

Marilyn smiled. "Every step counts. Healing isn't linear, but every step forward *matters.*"

Kyle added, "I've been... focusing on myself more. Journaling. Not dating. It's weird but... good."

Marilyn handed out the affirmation: *"I honor my progress, no matter how small."*

At The Corner Table

The energy at the table felt lighter, hopeful. For the first time in weeks, even Taryn smiled genuinely as they talked.

"You know," Kyle said, "we're kind of amazing. We've come... a long way."

Michelle laughed. "We really have."

Britney grinned. "I still feel like I'm at the start line, but... at least I *started*."

Taryn lifted her mug. "To starting... and keeping on going."

They clinked their mugs together, holding tight to the quiet victory of *progress*.

Michelle's Reflection

That night, Michelle journaled:

"I used to think strength meant having all the answers. But now I see—it's about showing up, even when you're scared. It's about building something new, step by shaky step. Watching Britney bloom... it reminds me how far I've come. And how much further we all can go."

She closed her journal, feeling—perhaps for the first time in her life—truly proud of the woman she was becoming.

Chapter 32

Britney's New Beginning

Britney sat cross-legged on her bed, her journal open across her knees. A half-melted candle flickered on her nightstand, casting warm shadows across the room. She tapped her pen against the page, smiling softly to herself.

She couldn't remember the last time she'd felt... part of something.

For weeks, she'd watched Taryn, Michelle, and Kyle from the sidelines, always feeling like the outsider looking in. But now? Now things felt different. She'd joined them at coffee. She'd shared her story in group. And tonight, for the first time in her life, she felt seen—not as someone needy or dramatic, but as someone who mattered.

She began to write, her handwriting looping across the page:

"I can't believe how much has changed. A few months ago, I thought I was completely alone. I thought no one would ever really understand me. But now... there's this group. And even though I was so scared at first, they didn't push me away. They listened. They welcomed me back. And tonight—when I shared about setting that boundary with my mom—they actually clapped for me. No one has ever clapped for me before for something like that."

She paused, biting her lip, then kept going:

"Michelle keeps saying healing is a process. That it's not about big leaps but small steps. I guess tonight I finally felt that. I felt... proud. I don't want to mess it up. I want to keep growing, even

when it's scary. For the first time in forever, I feel like maybe... just maybe... I'm not broken beyond repair."

Britney set her pen down, staring at the words for a long moment. A lump rose in her throat, but this time it wasn't sadness—it was relief.

She glanced at the tiny affirmation card Marilyn had handed out: *"I honor my progress, no matter how small."*

She whispered it out loud, letting the words sink in. "I honor my progress."

And for the first time in her life, she actually believed it.

Britney turned off the light, crawled under her blanket, and pulled her journal close to her chest. As she drifted off to sleep, a quiet hope fluttered inside her—the kind that comes from knowing you've finally taken your first real steps toward freedom.

Chapter 33

Kyle's Turning Point

Kyle sat at the kitchen table, flipping through old photos on his phone. There were pictures of him and Sid, then him and Natalie—smiling, laughing, wrapped up in what looked, on the surface, like love.

He sighed deeply. *It always looks good at the start,* he thought bitterly.

His phone buzzed—a text from Taryn: *"Group tonight? Thinking of you."*

He typed back: *"I'll be there."*

Thursday Night Group

Marilyn greeted everyone warmly, her calm presence anchoring the room as usual. "Tonight's focus: *Letting Go of the Fantasy.* One of the hardest parts of healing is accepting that the story we *wanted* is not the story we *have.*"

She glanced around the circle. "So many of us hold onto hope that our partners—or our families—will change. That if we just do the right things, everything will turn out okay. But real healing begins when we let go of that fantasy and accept what's true."

Rachel wiped her eyes. "That's... the hardest part for me. I keep thinking he'll realize I'm the best thing in his life. But... he never does."

Aaron added quietly, "I always pictured us growing old together. Now I'm starting over at 45."

Marilyn nodded. "It's heartbreaking. But freedom lies in facing the truth."

Kyle spoke next, his voice raw. "I think... I've been chasing the same woman over and over. Different faces, same patterns. And I kept believing... if I just *loved them enough,* they'd love me back the way I needed. But... they never did."

Britney chimed in, "That's why they say, same circus, different monkeys."

Everyone laughed. It was the perfect levity break.

Taryn looked at Kyle, eyes shining with understanding. "I've been there too."

Marilyn handed out the affirmation: *"I release the fantasy. I honor my reality and move forward in truth."*

At The Corner Table

Kyle stirred his coffee slowly. "It hit me tonight... I've been in love with *potential.* Not with who they really are."

Michelle nodded. "We all have. We see what we *hope* is there... and ignore what *is* there."

Taryn added, "It's like... we get addicted to hope. But hope alone isn't enough to build a life on."

Kyle smiled weakly. "I think... for the first time, I'm ready to let go. Not just of Sid, not just of Natalie. But of the whole *idea* that someone else will fix the empty parts of me."

Michelle grinned. "That's huge, Kyle. I'm so proud of you."

They raised their mugs, a silent toast to hard truths—and new beginnings.

Kyle's Journal

That night, Kyle opened his journal and wrote:

"Today, I made peace with the truth: love shouldn't hurt. I can love deeply, but I can't save someone who doesn't want to be saved. And I can't keep pouring from an empty cup. It's time to fill my own."

He closed the journal, a small, hopeful ache blooming in his chest.

Chapter 34

Naming the Abuse

The circle felt especially heavy tonight. The usual quiet hum of nervous chatter was absent, replaced by a kind of loaded stillness—as if everyone sensed that tonight would dig deeper than usual.

Marilyn, always calm and steady, looked around the room before she spoke. "We've spent a lot of time talking about boundaries, red flags, and patterns. But tonight, I want us to do something that might feel... difficult, but necessary."

She paused, meeting each pair of eyes in turn.

"I want us to call it what it is. Abuse."

A ripple of tension moved through the group. Taryn's stomach twisted. She'd said the word in her head before, but it still felt too sharp, too final.

Marilyn continued gently. "For many of us, it's easier to explain away the pain. To minimize. To think, 'It's not that bad,' or, 'It's not really abuse if they didn't hit me.' But abuse comes in many forms—emotional, verbal, spiritual, financial, and yes, physical. And naming it out loud is a powerful step toward reclaiming your truth."

She handed out slips of paper and pens. "Take a few minutes. Write down what you've experienced. Use whatever words feel right to you."

The room fell quiet except for the soft scratch of pens on paper. Taryn stared at the blank page, her hand frozen. Words circled in her head—words she'd buried for years:

- Manipulation
- Control
- Gaslighting
- Violence

Her throat tightened, but slowly, shakily, she began to write.

Around her, others were doing the same. Kyle tapped his pen nervously before writing something and shoving the paper into his pocket. Michelle's eyes glistened, her pen moving slowly but surely.

After a few minutes, Marilyn's voice broke the silence. "Would anyone like to share?"

A pause.

Then Rachel, her voice barely above a whisper. "I always thought... as long as he didn't hit me, it wasn't abuse. But now I realize... the constant belittling, the silent treatment, the control... that was abuse too."

Marilyn nodded. "Thank you for sharing that, Rachel. Emotional abuse can be just as damaging as physical abuse—and sometimes even harder to heal from because it's invisible."

Kyle spoke up next, his eyes downcast. "I wrote... betrayal. Undermining. Passive aggression. I didn't see it at first, but... she knew exactly how to make me feel worthless."

Michelle's voice shook slightly. "Mine... mine said I was too sensitive. That I made everything a big deal. He controlled every penny, every decision. And I thought that was normal for a while."

Marilyn's eyes were warm, her voice steady. "Thank you all for being brave enough to name it. That is a powerful step. Remember, abuse thrives in secrecy and silence. But when we name it, we begin to break its hold."

She handed out the affirmation card for the evening: *"My experience is real. My truth is valid. I am breaking free from shame."*

As the group wrapped up, Taryn sat in quiet reflection. Her paper lay in her lap, the words stark and undeniable. For the first time, she had written it down—not softened, not excused.

Abuse.

The word stared back at her like a mirror she could no longer turn away from.

And she knew—deep down—that her next step would be the hardest of all: saying it out loud.

Chapter 35

Breaking the Silence

The room was quieter than usual tonight. Taryn sat tracing her finger over the rim of her coffee cup, her journal resting on her lap. Marilyn's voice broke the stillness.

"We've all talked about the emotional and spiritual toll of abuse. But many of us carry silent scars too—the ones we've been too afraid or ashamed to name. Tonight, if anyone feels ready to share something deeper, this is a safe place."

For a long moment, no one spoke.

Taryn felt her pulse quicken. She looked down at her knees, covered now by jeans but forever marked by what had happened. A whisper from deep inside urged her: *It's time.*

She cleared her throat. "There's something I haven't told anyone here yet."

The group turned toward her, their eyes kind, patient.

She took a breath. "I've talked about Pete's manipulation, his verbal and emotional abuse... but what I haven't said is that he's also been physically abusive."

A hush fell.

"I tried to pretend it wasn't that bad. I minimized it—because that's what I had to do to survive. But there was one moment..." Her voice faltered, but she pressed on, feeling strength gather. "We were arguing, and for once, I stood my ground. I told him I wasn't going to back down—and that's when I saw it. That look. The one I'd seen before. I turned to run for the front door, but he caught me and threw me down so hard both my knees slammed into the tile floor."

She looked up, her eyes shining with tears. "I heard a pop. The pain was instant. I begged him for help. I told him he'd really hurt me this time. And you know what he did? He waited... and then threw a bag of frozen peas at me and said, 'Here—put this on the injury you gave yourself.'"

Gasps rippled around the circle. Michelle covered her mouth, her eyes brimming.

"For weeks, I could barely walk. My knees turned blue and stayed bruised for months. And still, Pete rewrote the story. Told me I fell. Told me it was my fault." Taryn's voice trembled. "And the worst part? I started to believe him. I convinced myself that if I just stayed quiet, if I didn't push back, it wouldn't happen again."

She wiped her eyes, her voice steadying. "But deep down, I knew the truth. And God knew it too. That's what kept me from completely losing myself. Even when Pete said I was crazy, even when he made me feel invisible—I knew God saw me. *'The Lord is close to the brokenhearted and saves those who are crushed in spirit.'*" She smiled faintly. "Psalm 34:18 has gotten me through a lot."

Marilyn's eyes glistened as she leaned forward. "Taryn, thank you. That took incredible courage to share. And let me be clear: you did not deserve what happened. Not any of it. You have survived so much, and you are walking testimony that God's strength is made perfect in our weakness."

Kyle's voice was thick with emotion. "I'm so sorry, Taryn. That... that's just evil. I'm glad you're here. I'm glad you're safe."

Michelle reached over, her hand warm and firm. "You are one of the bravest women I've ever met. Thank you for trusting us."

Marilyn handed out the evening's affirmation card: *"My wounds do not define me. My faith strengthens me. I am reclaiming my voice, one truth at a time."*

Taryn took a deep breath, her tears falling freely now—not just tears of pain, but of release. And in that small room, with her friends around her and her heart open at last, she felt a quiet shift.

For the first time, she was no longer just surviving—she was healing.

Quiet Reflections: The Morning After

Taryn sat by her bedroom window the next morning, a cup of tea cradled between her palms. The house was still, bathed in soft morning light, but her heart felt different—lighter somehow. As she stared out at the tree branches swaying gently, her mind replayed the night before.

She had spoken her truth. Out loud. To people who didn't shrink away or doubt her but instead sat with her pain and believed her.

She opened her journal and let the words flow:

Last night, I named it. I said out loud what I've hidden in the deepest corners of my soul. And somehow, I feel... free. Not because the pain disappeared—but because the shame started to lose its grip. For the first time in years, I remembered: my voice matters.

She smiled faintly, tears prickling her eyes.

God, thank you. Thank you for giving me the courage to speak. Thank you for surrounding me with people who listen with compassion, who don't judge or dismiss my story. I know now what Your Word says is true: 'You will know the truth, and the truth will set you free.' (John 8:32).

She closed her journal and whispered into the quiet, "I'm not done healing. But I am no longer hiding."

And with that, Taryn stood, took a deep breath, and stepped into her day—head held a little higher, her heart a little stronger.

Chapter 36

Slipping Back In

Taryn stared at the clock on her apartment wall. 9:42 p.m. The apartment was dark, save for the faint glow of a streetlight filtering through the blinds. Her suitcase sat in the corner, still packed from her weekend at Pete's.

She had told herself it was just a visit. Just a few days to help him get settled after his diagnosis. But now, back in her apartment, it didn't feel right. It didn't feel… like home.

The silence pressed in around her, heavy and suffocating. She clutched her phone in both hands, scrolling back through Pete's recent messages:

Thank you for being here, Taryn. I don't deserve you.

I don't know how I'd get through this without your help.

You have always been my angel. God knew what He was doing when He gave me you.

Each one made her stomach twist. She knew the pattern—oh, how well she knew the pattern. The love bombing. The guilt. The tenderness that only lasted as long as it took to hook her back in.

And yet… it worked.

Her mind wandered back to the moment she'd stepped into their old house that weekend. Pete had looked frail, sitting there in his recliner, his voice shaky as he told her about the diagnosis. His eyes had welled up with tears—real or performative, she wasn't sure anymore—and in that moment, her heart had splintered.

"I can't face this alone, Taryn," he'd whispered, gripping her hand so tightly it hurt. "I need you."

It was everything she'd ever wanted to hear. And everything she'd feared.

She squeezed her eyes shut now, tears spilling down her cheeks. How many times had she dreamed of breaking free—of standing on her own, of reclaiming her life? How many times had she sworn *never again*?

And here she was. Teetering on the edge. Letting Pete quilt trap her again.

Her phone buzzed, jolting her out of her thoughts. It was a text from Michelle:

Hey, just checking in. How are you feeling tonight? Need to talk?

Taryn stared at the message, her thumb hovering over the keys. What could she even say? That she felt like she was drowning all over again? That despite everything she'd worked for, she was slipping right back into the same old trap?

She wiped her tears and started typing:

I'm okay. Just… helping Pete through this. I'll be fine.

But it felt like a lie. And before she hit send, she deleted it.

Her eyes darted around the apartment—the sparse furniture, the walls she'd painted with hope, the little signs of independence she'd worked so hard to build. And yet… none of it felt real anymore.

She thought about Kenny and Kate. About how they'd looked at her with pride when she'd made the decision for them to move out. About the strength she'd shown them. Was she about to undo all of that?

Her phone buzzed again.

We're here for you, no matter what, Michelle had written. *You're stronger than you know.*

Taryn let out a shaky breath, her thumb finally settling on a reply:

I don't know what I'm doing anymore. I'm so tired.

She hit send and sat back, staring at the ceiling, her tears coming harder now. The apartment around her blurred, her vision clouded by the ache of confusion and guilt.

A few days later, she found herself standing at Pete's front door again, suitcase in hand.

"I told you I'd come by and help," she said, her voice hesitant as he opened the door.

Pete smiled softly, stepping aside to let her in. "You're a gift from God, Taryn. You are my angel. I mean that."

She told herself it was just for the week. Just until he got through his next round of appointments. But one week turned into two… and then three. Her apartment sat empty, gathering dust, while Pete's house filled up again with her things—her clothes in the drawers, her shoes by the door.

And just like that, Taryn's new chapter faded into the background. The woman who had once stood so firm—who had once dared to believe she could break free—began to fold back into the life she'd tried so hard to escape.

One night, as she lay in bed next to Pete, staring at the ceiling in the dark, she whispered a prayer.

"God... is this really what You want? Or am I just too afraid to let go?"

But the only answer was the quiet hum of the ceiling fan, spinning endlessly above her.

Thursday Night Group

Even though Taryn wasn't there, her absence filled the room.

Michelle brought it up first. "Taryn's... struggling. Pete's pulling her back in."

Marilyn nodded, her eyes full of empathy. "It's a heavy pull. Guilt, fear, hope—it all collides. Let's send her love and strength tonight."

The group murmured their agreement, a quiet undercurrent of prayer and hope circling the room.

Marilyn's topic for the night: *"The Relapse: When We Return to Familiar Pain."*

She began, "We often talk about progress as a straight line, but healing isn't linear. Sometimes we take huge steps forward—and then a few steps back. That doesn't mean we've failed. It means we're still learning."

Rachel asked, "How do you stop yourself from going back... when everything in you wants to believe *this time* will be different?"

Marilyn answered softly, "You build a community. You stay honest with yourself. And even if you do go back... you don't stay blind. You keep your eyes open."

Kyle whispered, "Taryn's eyes are open now. That's... something."

Michelle added, "I just want her to know... no matter what happens, we're still here."

Marilyn smiled. "That's what real love looks like."

Chapter 37

A New Season for Michelle

Michelle stood at her classroom's window, watching her students laugh and play at recess. The autumn breeze danced through the playground, scattering golden leaves like tiny, swirling dancers. She hugged her sweater closer around her and allowed herself a rare, lingering smile. It struck her how much her own life mirrored this season—letting go of the old, stepping into something new and vibrant.

Her phone vibrated on the desk. A text from Britney: *"Just had my first job interview! Can we talk later?"*

Michelle's heart swelled with pride. Britney's progress felt almost like watching one of her students blossom—tentative at first, but gaining strength each week.

She typed back: *"Yes! So proud of you. Let's catch up tonight."*

She slipped the phone back into her desk and let her gaze drift to the playground again. For a long time, she'd thought freedom was something for other people. But now, here she was—free, standing tall in her own life.

Thursday Night Group

The chairs filled up quickly that evening, but Taryn's usual spot stayed empty. Her absence had become routine now, but it left a quiet ache, especially for Kyle and Michelle.

Marilyn welcomed everyone and introduced tonight's theme: *"The Gifts of Freedom."*

"When we break free from toxic patterns," Marilyn began, "we don't just survive—we open ourselves to new gifts. Peace. Joy. Confidence. And sometimes... new beginnings we never imagined."

She paused to look around the room. "I want to hear from each of you tonight. What gifts have come to you—no matter how small—since you began this journey?"

Aaron said, "I'm finally sleeping through the night. That feels like a gift."

Rachel added, "I started painting again. I forgot how much I loved it."

Britney looked hesitant but spoke up. "I applied for two jobs. I've never done that before. And... I think I might actually get one."

The room erupted in applause.

Michelle's turn came, and she took a deep breath. "I've been feeling... proud. I'm managing my own money, raising my kids, doing work I love. And... I'm starting to feel like *me* again."

She smiled, and her eyes shimmered with emotion. "And... I've been mentoring Britney. That, too, feels like a gift."

More clapping and warm smiles circled the room.

Marilyn's face was full of pride. "That's the beauty of healing. We reclaim parts of ourselves we thought were lost."

The affirmation that night: *"I am worthy of every good thing that comes my way."*

At The Corner Table

Kyle, Michelle, and Britney gathered in their familiar booth, the hum of coffee machines and laughter blending into their ritual of safety and honesty.

Britney took a long sip of her coffee. "I still feel... fragile. Like one bad day could break me all over again."

Michelle smiled kindly. "That's normal. But look at you—every week, you get stronger. Even recognizing that fear is progress."

Kyle leaned in. "I've been thinking... when we first met, I didn't think *any* of us would make it this far. But we have. We're proof that healing's messy—but possible."

Britney's eyes glistened. "Do you think Taryn will get there too?"

A long pause.

Michelle sighed. "I hope so. But... we have to remember—it's her journey. We can't walk it for her. We can't tell her what choice to make. Only Taryn can make that choice for herself. Remember we care, we don't carry."

Kyle added, "She knows we're here. That counts for something."

They clinked their mugs together—this time in quiet gratitude for the healing they *had* found, and hope for the healing still to come.

Michelle's Evening Reflection

After tucking Kitty and Kevin into bed and cleaning up the dinner mess, Michelle settled onto her couch, wrapping herself in a soft blanket with a cup of chamomile tea. The house was quiet now, peaceful in a way it hadn't been for years.

She opened her journal and began to write:

"I never thought I'd feel this way again—safe, steady, proud. There's still hard days, sure. But today, I realized something important: I am no longer waiting for someone else to save me. I am my own rescue. Watching Britney grow, watching Kyle find his strength... it's beautiful. We're not just survivors—we're builders of new lives. And maybe, just maybe, that's the greatest gift of all."

Her phone buzzed. A text from Britney: *"Thank you for everything. I don't know where I'd be without you."*

Michelle smiled, her eyes filling with grateful tears. She replied: *"You're doing the hard work, Brit. I'm just cheering you on. You've got this."*

She leaned back, watching the flicker of candlelight dance across her living room wall. For the first time in a long time, she felt at peace—a deep, abiding peace that wasn't tied to anyone else.

It was hers alone.

At The Corner Table

Kyle, Michelle, and Britney met for coffee, the absence of Taryn palpable.

"I hate that she's going through this," Michelle said, stirring her drink.

Kyle frowned. "I get it though. It's... so easy to slip back when you're scared and lonely."

Britney was quiet, then said, "She's strong. She'll figure it out."

Michelle smiled at her. "You're stronger than you know too, Brit."

They clinked mugs, this time as a prayer for Taryn, sending strength across the miles.

Taryn's Quiet Resolve

That night, Taryn lay in bed, staring at the ceiling. Pete's breathing beside her was slow, steady—he had fallen asleep mid-conversation, like always.

She rolled over, clutching her pillow, eyes stinging with tears.

"God... help me. Help me know what to do."

She didn't have answers yet. But she knew one thing: the ache in her chest wouldn't go away just because she'd returned. Healing wasn't something Pete could promise her. It was something she had to find for herself.

And maybe... just maybe... she still would.

Chapter 38

The Invitation

Kyle sat alone at his kitchen table, scrolling through his texts. A familiar ache settled in his chest as he reread Taryn's latest message: *"Thanks for checking in. Things are complicated right now. I'll come back to group soon."*

He sighed and tossed his phone onto the table. The apartment felt emptier these days—Natalie was long gone, and despite the heartbreak, Kyle felt... relieved. For the first time in years, he wasn't tied to anyone. But the silence pressed on him, reminding him that healing could be lonely too.

His phone buzzed again, this time a group text from Michelle: *"Coffee shop tonight? 7 pm? Britney's bringing cupcakes!"*

A small smile crept across Kyle's face. *These are my people,* he thought. *And I need them tonight.*

At The Corner Table

The little café was warm and inviting, the windows fogged up from the chill outside. Michelle, Britney, and Kyle gathered around their table, the familiar clink of mugs and low hum of conversation filling the space.

Britney set down a pink bakery box. "Okay, these are the best cupcakes in town, and I will not be argued with."

Michelle laughed. "Confidence! I love it."

Kyle grinned. "I'll be the judge of that."

As they dug in, the conversation turned more serious.

Britney glanced at Kyle. "How are you doing... really? We haven't talked much since Natalie."

Kyle wiped a crumb from his lip and sighed. "Honestly? Better than I expected. It hurts, yeah. But it's... different this time. I'm not blaming myself. I'm starting to see the patterns, and I don't want to go back there."

Michelle smiled, pride shining in her eyes. "That's real growth, Kyle."

He nodded, though his eyes looked far away. "I just wish... Taryn could see it too. That she deserves better."

Britney leaned in. "Have you heard from her?"

Kyle's face softened. "A little. She's... hanging on. Says things are complicated."

Michelle shook her head gently. "It breaks my heart. But like we've said—she has to want it for herself."

There was a long pause, each of them sitting in the quiet understanding of how hard it was to walk away from familiar pain.

Meanwhile, Taryn's World

At home, Taryn sat on the couch, flipping through a photo album. Old pictures of her kids—Brandon, Kate, and Kenny—smiling at birthdays, school plays, vacations. Her heart ached as she traced their young faces with her fingertips.

Pete's voice rang out from the kitchen, cheerful but sharp-edged: "Did you pick up my prescription today?"

Taryn closed the album and stood, forcing a smile as she walked into the other room. "Yes, it's on the counter."

Pete kissed her cheek lightly. "You're a good woman, Taryn. I don't know what I'd do without you."

She swallowed hard. *He always knows just what to say when I'm slipping away,* she thought.

Later that evening, as Pete fell asleep in his chair, Taryn scrolled through her phone, lingering on a picture from the group chat—Kyle, Michelle, and Britney at the coffee shop, laughing over cupcakes.

She stared at it for a long time, tears welling in her eyes. Part of her wanted to throw the phone across the room... but another part longed to be back there, in that warmth, in that truth.

Her finger hovered over the keyboard. Finally, she typed: *"Miss you all. Hope to see you soon."*

Group Night: A Surprise Visitor

The next Thursday, Michelle and Kyle sat in their usual seats as Marilyn began the group session. They were deep in conversation about *self-worth* when the door opened... and Taryn stepped in.

The room fell quiet for a moment, then erupted into warm welcomes. Michelle's eyes filled with tears as she hugged her tightly. "We've missed you so much."

Kyle grinned, clapping Taryn gently on the back. "Good to see you, friend."

Britney practically bounced in her seat. "We saved your spot!"

Taryn looked overwhelmed but grateful as she settled in. "I... I wasn't sure if I'd come. But something in me just... needed to be here tonight."

Marilyn smiled, her eyes kind. "We're so glad you're here, Taryn. Welcome back."

That night's topic: *"Returning to Yourself."*

Marilyn's voice was gentle but strong. "Sometimes, life pulls us away from our own center. Toxic relationships, guilt, fear—they can all cloud our vision of who we really are. But no matter how far we drift, it's never too late to come home to ourselves."

Taryn listened, tears silently streaming down her face. Every word felt like it was spoken just for her.

When it was her turn to share, she hesitated, then said softly, "I've been... lost. I thought going back would make things right. But it hasn't. I don't even know who I am anymore."

Michelle squeezed her hand. "That's okay. The fact that you're here means... you're finding your way back."

Taryn nodded, her lips trembling. "I hope so. I really do."

Marilyn passed around the affirmation: *"No matter how far I wander, I can always return to myself."*

At The Corner Table (Again)

After group, the four of them gathered once more at their beloved corner table. There was an extra sense of tenderness that night, everyone savoring the fact that they were all together again.

Taryn stirred her tea slowly. "I don't know what's going to happen next. But... being here tonight reminded me I'm not alone."

Kyle nodded. "You never were. And you never will be."

Britney added, "We're your people. We've got you."

Michelle smiled, her heart swelling with love for these brave, broken, healing souls. "One step at a time, Taryn. You're stronger than you think."

They lifted their mugs once more, a toast not just to friendship, but to the long, winding road back to themselves.

And in that quiet corner of the coffee shop, for the first time in a long time, Taryn let herself hope.

Chapter 39

Shifting Ground

The week after Taryn's return to group was different. There was a quiet hum of renewed energy among them—a cautious hope. Michelle and Kyle had been texting with her every day, checking in, offering small encouragements. Britney had even sent a funny meme about "group therapy besties," and Taryn had responded with her first genuine laugh in a long time.

But in Taryn's house, things weren't as hopeful.

She sat on her bed late one night, staring at the ceiling. Pete had been showering her with affection since she mentioned going back to group—bringing her flowers, cooking dinner, quoting Scripture about forgiveness and family. To anyone looking from the outside, it was picture-perfect.

But to Taryn, it felt hollow. Familiar. *Too familiar.*

She rubbed her temples, exhausted by the emotional whiplash. She had seen this pattern before: the charm, the promises, the love-bombing—and then the inevitable crash back into control and abuse. The cycle was so predictable now that it was almost eerie.

Her phone buzzed with a message from Michelle: *"How's your heart tonight?"*

Taryn stared at it for a long moment, then typed back: *"Tired. But grateful for you."*

A pause. Then another message: *"You don't have to carry it alone anymore. I mean it."*

Taryn's eyes welled with tears. She whispered into the darkness, "I don't know how much longer I can keep doing this."

Thursday Night Group

That week's meeting was quieter, more intimate. Marilyn welcomed everyone with her usual warmth but with an added seriousness tonight. "Our topic: *'Recognizing the Patterns.'*"

She glanced at the group. "We've talked about cycles of abuse, but tonight, we're going to look at how those patterns *pull us back in,* even when we know better. And more importantly—how to *interrupt* them."

Kyle sighed. "It's like... every time I think I've broken free, I find myself drawn to the same type of person again. I swear, it's like I have a magnet for narcissists."

Britney nodded. "Me too, but with my mom. I feel like... no matter what boundaries I set, she finds a way to push through."

Taryn spoke up next, her voice shaking slightly. "It's the charm that gets me. Pete knows exactly what to say. Exactly how to *make me hope again.* And even though I know it's part of the cycle... it's so hard to resist that tiny voice that says, 'Maybe this time it's real.'"

Michelle squeezed her hand. "I know that voice. I've heard it too. But Taryn... you're stronger now. You're seeing it for what it is. That's huge."

Marilyn added gently, "Awareness is the first step. Once you see the pattern, you *can't unsee it.* And while that's painful... it's also the beginning of real change."

They passed around the affirmation: *"I deserve love that does not hurt."*

At The Corner Table

Later that night, they settled into their booth, their safe haven. The café was quieter than usual, and for a while, they sat in a comfortable silence, sipping their drinks and just *being.*

Kyle finally broke the silence. "Do you guys ever... worry that healing is just another kind of trap? Like... we get better, but we're still waiting for the other shoe to drop?"

Michelle thought for a moment. "I think that's just... part of the trauma. We're so used to chaos that peace feels unnatural at first. But over time... I think it *can* become our new normal."

Britney leaned forward. "I'm starting to feel that. Like... baby steps. But I'm noticing the change."

Taryn smiled faintly. "I'm not there yet. But tonight... tonight felt like a step."

Michelle beamed at her. "It *was* a step. And we'll keep taking them—together."

They lifted their mugs one more time, their silent toast a prayer for progress, for strength, and for the courage to keep walking the path—even when it hurt.

Taryn's Late-Night Moment

At home, long after Pete had gone to bed, Taryn stood by the window, staring out into the night. The streetlights cast long shadows across the pavement, and the cool air seeped through the crack in the window.

She whispered aloud, "God, help me break free. For good this time."

Her heart pounded, and for the first time in a long while, she felt... determined. The path ahead was still foggy, but somewhere deep inside her, a seed of courage had been planted—and it was beginning to grow.

She turned from the window, her eyes catching on her journal. She opened it, writing in shaky but certain letters:

"I am worthy of real love. I am worthy of peace. I am worthy of freedom."

She closed the journal, exhaled deeply, and crawled into bed—hope flickering quietly in her chest.

Chapter 40

Michelle's Breakthrough

Michelle sat at her kitchen table surrounded by bills, her laptop open and glowing in the dim evening light. The kids were playing upstairs, and for once, there was no tension—just the quiet hum of a home at peace.

She clicked "Submit" on her last online payment and leaned back with a deep sigh. It was the first time since leaving Matt that she'd fully caught up on her finances. No overdue notices. No secret panic. Just... handled.

She couldn't help but laugh a little, the sound catching in her throat. It wasn't flashy or dramatic, but this was victory. *Her* victory.

Her phone rang. Britney's name flashed on the screen.

"Hey Brit!" Michelle answered, her voice warm.

"Michelle... I got the job!" Britney's voice was breathless with excitement. "It's part-time at the bookstore downtown, but it's a start!"

Michelle clapped her hand over her heart. "Oh, Brit—that's amazing! I'm so proud of you."

"You... you helped me believe I could do it," Britney said, her voice cracking. "I couldn't have done this without you."

Michelle blinked back tears. "Yes, you could. You *did*. I'm just lucky to cheer you on."

They made plans to celebrate soon, and when Michelle hung up, she sat for a moment, staring at the tidy pile of paid bills and her now-quiet phone.

This was her life now—stable, growing, *hers*.

Group Night: Owning Strength

That week at group, the circle buzzed with quiet excitement. Marilyn had asked everyone to bring something that represented their personal growth—a symbol of how far they'd come.

Aaron brought a pair of running shoes. "I started jogging again," he said, holding them up. "They remind me that I'm still moving forward, even on days I want to give up."

Rachel held up a paintbrush. "I finished my first canvas in years," she said, smiling shyly. "It's messy but... it's *mine*."

Britney grinned and held up her bookstore nametag. The group erupted in cheers and applause, making her beam with pride.

When it was Michelle's turn, she pulled out her classroom lanyard and a tiny, worn-out piggy bank. "The lanyard is for my job—because I'm finally back in a place where I *thrive*. The piggy bank... that's for learning to manage my own money. I never thought I could do it without Matt, but here I am."

Marilyn smiled. "Powerful. Tangible reminders of reclaiming your independence."

Everyone turned to Taryn, who sat with her hands clasped tightly in her lap.

She hesitated, then opened her purse and pulled out her journal. "This... is where I write everything I *can't* say out loud. It's been my lifeline these last few weeks."

Kyle leaned forward, his voice gentle. "That's huge, Taryn. Writing is powerful. It means you're facing the truth."

Marilyn nodded. "And truth is the first step toward lasting change."

The affirmation that night: *"Every small step forward is a victory."*

The Coffee Shop: A Celebration

After group, the now-traditional coffee shop meetup felt lighter than it had in months. Britney set down a little cake from the bakery and grinned. "We're celebrating *everything* tonight."

They laughed and shared updates—Britney's new job, Kyle's continued self-reflection, Michelle's steady rise.

Taryn sat quietly for a moment, then said softly, "It's strange... I came tonight thinking I was the weakest one here. But I look around this table, and... we've *all* done hard things."

Michelle smiled. "That's the truth. And Taryn... you're stronger than you know. Coming back to group, showing up—that's not weakness. That's courage."

Kyle lifted his mug. "To courage."

They all clinked mugs, their eyes shining with gratitude and hard-earned strength.

Michelle's Quiet Night

At home later, Michelle tucked Kitty and Kevin into bed and lingered at the doorway, watching them sleep. Her heart ached with fierce love—and pride. They were thriving too, safe and happy because she had fought for them, fought for herself.

She walked back downstairs, poured a glass of wine, and sat on the porch, staring up at the stars.

She whispered into the night, "Thank you, God. For second chances. For freedom. For *this*."

She let the quiet wrap around her, no longer afraid of silence. It wasn't empty now—it was full of peace, of promise.

Michelle closed her eyes, a smile playing at her lips. Tomorrow was another day. Another victory waiting to unfold.

And she was ready for it

Chapter 41

Kyle's Full Circle Moment

Kyle sat alone in his car outside his apartment, gripping the steering wheel. The engine was off, but the weight of his thoughts felt heavier than any key he could turn.

He stared at the text on his phone—Natalie again. *"Let's talk. I miss you."*

His chest tightened. Part of him—*the old part*—ached to respond. To rush back to that familiar dance of attention and validation. But another part of him, quieter but growing stronger, whispered, *No. Not again.*

He let the phone drop into the console and leaned his head back, eyes closed, breathing deeply. *What am I even doing?* he asked himself. *What do I want?*

His thoughts wandered to Michelle and Britney—their laughter, their progress, their strength. And Taryn... her quiet fight to pull herself out of the same pit he kept falling into.

Kyle exhaled sharply. "It's time," he whispered to himself.

Thursday Night Group: Facing the Mirror

That week's group was packed. Marilyn stood in the center of the circle, holding a small mirror.

"Tonight's topic," she said, "is *'Facing Ourselves.'*"

She walked around the room slowly. "It's easy to focus on what others have done to us. And that's valid—we have to name and confront abuse. But healing also means asking the hard question: *What have we allowed? What do we need to change within ourselves to break free?*"

The room was silent, thick with the weight of her words.

Marilyn held up the mirror. "Tonight, I want you to look at your reflection—not with shame, but with honesty and compassion. We are not to blame for others' abuse. But we are responsible for our healing."

She handed the mirror to Kyle first.

He stared into it, his throat tight. "I see... someone who keeps choosing the same pain over and over. Someone who... is scared to be alone. Scared to let go."

His voice wavered, but he held Marilyn's gaze. "But I also see... someone who *wants* to change. Who's *trying*."

The group nodded, murmuring quiet support.

Michelle took the mirror next. "I see... someone who thought she was weak but learned she's strong. Someone who's still healing... but proud of how far she's come."

Taryn's turn. She looked at her reflection, her eyes glossy with tears. "I see... someone who's tired. So tired. But... someone who's starting to believe she deserves more."

Marilyn smiled, her voice soft but strong. "That's where it begins."

The affirmation that night: *"I am both worthy and capable of healing."*

The Coffee Shop: The Hard Talk

Later, at their booth, the conversation turned serious.

Kyle toyed with his coffee cup, eyes down. "I need to tell you guys something. Natalie's been texting. A lot."

Michelle's eyes widened slightly, but she kept her tone calm. "And?"

Kyle looked up, meeting her gaze. "And... I didn't respond. I *wanted* to. But... I didn't."

Britney grinned. "That's huge, Kyle."

Kyle sighed. "Yeah, but... it's hard. Part of me still feels like... what if I'm making a mistake? What if I *miss* something good?"

Michelle reached across the table, placing her hand over his. "Kyle... wanting love doesn't make you weak. But *settling for crumbs* when you deserve the whole feast—that's what keeps us stuck. You're doing the hard thing right now. That *is* strength."

Kyle swallowed hard, emotion tightening his throat. "Thanks, guys. Really. I don't know where I'd be without you."

Taryn added quietly, "We're in this together. Always."

They clinked their mugs again, that familiar silent promise holding them steady.

Kyle's Turning Point

Later that night, alone in his apartment, Kyle stared at his phone again. Natalie's last message glowed on the screen: *"I miss your smile. Let's try again."*

He sat there for a long time, heart pounding. Then, slowly, deliberately, he deleted the thread. Every message. Every photo. Every trace.

He set the phone down and let out a breath that felt like it had been stuck inside him for years.

For the first time in a long time, he felt... free.

He grabbed a pen and paper and wrote:

"Tonight, I chose me. It hurts. But it's also the bravest thing I've done in a long time."

He tucked the note into his journal and climbed into bed, pulling the blankets up to his chin. The quiet no longer felt like punishment.

It felt like peace.

And for now, that was enough.

Chapter 42

Familiar Enough to Embrace

Taryn stood at her kitchen sink, staring out the window as dusk fell over the backyard. Pete's voice echoed from the living room, booming with forced cheerfulness as he watched a game show. On the counter beside her was a vase of fresh roses—Pete's latest peace offering.

She picked up one of the roses and touched its soft petals, feeling the sharp prick of a hidden thorn beneath. *Perfect,* she thought. *Beautiful on the outside. Painful underneath.*

Her phone buzzed with a message from Michelle: *"Just thinking about you. Hope you're okay tonight."*

Taryn didn't reply right away. She stared at the screen, her thumb hovering, her heart aching. Finally, she typed: *"I'm here. Hanging on."*

She stared at those words. *Hanging on.* It didn't feel like enough anymore.

Group Night: Permission to Feel

Marilyn greeted everyone warmly that week, her tone gentle. "Tonight we're talking about something many of us forget—*permission to feel.*"

She looked around the room. "Abuse numbs us. It teaches us to shrink our feelings, to hide them, to question them. But healing means giving ourselves permission to feel everything—anger, sadness, fear, even joy."

She passed around slips of paper and pens. "Write down a feeling you've been pushing away."

Taryn's pen trembled in her hand. She stared at the blank slip for a long time before writing a single word: *Grief.*

Michelle wrote: *Relief.*

Kyle hesitated, then scrawled: *Loneliness.*

When it came time to share, Marilyn asked gently, "Taryn, would you like to start?"

Taryn looked down at her paper, her throat tight. "Grief," she whispered. "I've been grieving... everything. The life I thought I had. The marriage I wanted. The woman I used to be."

Her voice cracked, and tears slipped down her cheeks. "And I think... I've been afraid to let myself feel it all, because... what if it breaks me?"

Marilyn leaned in. "Feeling grief doesn't break you, Taryn. *It frees you.* You're already carrying the weight. Letting it surface is how you begin to set it down."

Michelle added softly, "It's okay to mourn what we lost—even if it was never what we deserved."

The room nodded in quiet understanding.

Kyle spoke next. "Loneliness. Even though I've walked away from toxic stuff... I'm scared I'll always feel alone."

Britney piped up, "You're not alone now."

Kyle smiled, gratitude shining in his eyes. "Thanks, Brit."

Michelle's turn. "Relief. I... I've been feeling guilty about how *good* life feels lately. Like, shouldn't I still be struggling? But... I'm not. And it feels... weird."

Marilyn smiled. "You're allowed to feel good, Michelle. *That's the point of healing.*"

The affirmation that night: *"I honor my feelings. They are valid and safe to express."*

After Group: An Honest Talk

Back at the coffee shop, their table felt more sacred than ever. Taryn sipped her tea slowly, her eyes distant.

"Pete's been... good lately," she began. "Really good. Flowers. Dinners. Sweet words."

Kyle exchanged a look with Michelle, both staying quiet.

Taryn exhaled. "But... I don't trust it. I know the cycle. I *feel* the tension under it all. And I hate that even when it's good... I can't relax."

Michelle reached over, squeezing her hand. "That's because your gut knows the truth, Taryn. You *deserve* to feel safe all the time, not just when he's performing."

Kyle nodded. "You've come too far to settle for breadcrumbs again."

Taryn's eyes brimmed with tears. "I know. I just... I feel trapped."

Britney chimed in, her voice soft but certain. "We're not going anywhere. You're not alone."

For the first time that night, Taryn smiled—small, but real. "Thank you. All of you."

Taryn's Private Moment

Later, alone in her bedroom, Taryn pulled out her journal. She ran her fingers over the pages, then began to write:

"Tonight I admitted my grief out loud. I let myself feel it. And even though it hurts... it feels like I cracked open a window after years of suffocating. I don't know what's next. But I know I can't keep pretending. Not anymore."

She closed the journal, exhaled shakily, and whispered into the darkness, "Help me, God. Please... help me."

The night was silent in response, but somewhere deep inside, a quiet strength stirred—a flicker of hope, stubborn and persistent.

And Taryn knew: the cracks appearing now weren't a sign of breaking.

They were the first signs of light getting in.

Chapter 43

Crossroads and Courage

Michelle's classroom was buzzing with the sweet chaos of second graders practicing for their spring concert. She stood at the front of the room, waving her arms in mock-conducting while Kitty, her daughter, sat at the back coloring quietly—an after-school tagalong.

As the kids filed out, waving and chattering, Michelle leaned back against her desk, feeling a rush of gratitude. *This,* she thought, *is what freedom looks like. A life I built myself.*

Kitty ran up and hugged her legs. "Mama, can we get ice cream?"

Michelle laughed. "You bet, baby."

Her phone buzzed just as she was locking up—Taryn's name flashing across the screen. Michelle's stomach fluttered; she hadn't heard much from her that week.

T: *"Can we meet tonight? Just us?"*

Michelle's heart ached. *Of course.*

Later That Night: The Hard Truth

They met at their usual coffee shop, tucked into a quiet corner. Taryn looked tired—exhausted, really—but there was a clarity in her eyes Michelle hadn't seen in a while.

"I'm so glad you texted," Michelle said gently. "How are you?"

Taryn stared at her tea, fingers wrapped tightly around the mug. "I've been... lying to myself."

Michelle stayed quiet, waiting.

"I wanted to believe Pete had changed. I *wanted* to believe that maybe... if I just worked harder, prayed harder... it could all be different."

Her eyes welled with tears. "But it's not different. The cycle's back. The mood swings. The control. The little jabs. It's like... the more I hope, the harder I fall."

Michelle reached across the table, her grip firm. "I'm so sorry, Taryn. I know how hard it is to face that."

Taryn's voice dropped to a whisper. "And the worst part? I feel... ashamed. I told everyone I was done. I was *so proud* of leaving. And now... I feel like I failed."

Michelle's eyes were fierce. "No. Don't even *go there*. You didn't fail. You're human. We *all* want to believe in love. We all want to hope people can change. That's not weakness—that's your beautiful, open heart."

Taryn sniffled, wiping her eyes. "I don't know what to do next."

Michelle squeezed her hand. "One step at a time. You don't have to have all the answers tonight. But you *do* have people who love you. Who will hold you up until you can stand strong again."

Taryn gave a shaky smile. "Thank you. I needed to hear that."

Kyle's Quiet Night

Meanwhile, Kyle sat at his kitchen table, flipping through an old photo album. Pictures of him and Sidney on vacations, at family parties, laughing together.

He stared at the images, feeling a strange mix of sadness and relief. He realized something powerful: *I don't miss her. I miss the idea of love.*

He closed the album, setting it aside like he was finally closing a chapter. He grabbed his journal and wrote:

"Healing is lonely sometimes. But it's better than being lost in someone else's chaos. Tonight, I choose peace over patterns."

He looked out the window, feeling the quiet settle over him—and for the first time, it didn't feel like emptiness.

It felt like space.

Group Night: Declaring Strength

At group that week, Marilyn's topic was bold: *"Declaring Our Strengths."*

"We spend so much time talking about what's broken," Marilyn began. "Tonight, I want to shift that. Let's name what's *strong* in us—what we've reclaimed, what we've *earned* through this journey."

Rachel spoke first. "I'm strong because... I finally believe my voice matters."

Aaron added, "I'm strong because I walked away from someone who didn't respect me—and I'm still standing."

Britney beamed. "I'm strong because I'm building a new life—and loving it."

Kyle took a deep breath. "I'm strong because... I'm learning to be okay alone. And I'm proud of that."

Michelle's eyes glowed. "I'm strong because I broke free—and I'm raising my kids in peace."

All eyes turned to Taryn.

She hesitated, tears welling up again. But then she spoke, voice trembling but true: "I'm strong because... even though I stumbled, I came back. I showed up. And I'm still here."

The room filled with quiet, powerful applause.

Marilyn smiled, her eyes shining. "That's real strength, Taryn. And you're not alone."

The affirmation that night: *"My strength is my truth—and it grows every day."*

Closing Scene: A New Dawn

That night, Taryn sat by her bedroom window, watching the moon rise. She felt raw, cracked open—but also... lighter.

Her phone buzzed: a simple heart emoji from Michelle, and a thumbs-up from Kyle in their group chat.

Taryn smiled through her tears, whispered to herself, "One step at a time."

And as the moon climbed higher in the sky, she let herself believe—just for tonight—that hope was still worth holding onto.

Chapter 44

When the Mask Slips

The early days of spring brought a deceptive warmth to Taryn's world. Pete had been in full-on charm mode again—lavish breakfasts, love notes tucked into her purse, and prayers at dinner that sounded almost like poetry.

But deep down, Taryn felt it—a creeping, gnawing tension that never fully left her body.

It was Friday night, and Pete was watching TV when his phone buzzed on the table. He didn't move to pick it up, and curiosity got the better of Taryn. She glanced at the screen: a message from a name she didn't recognize. Her stomach dropped.

"Who's that?" she asked lightly, her heart pounding.

Pete's face shifted—just for a flash—but it was enough. His mask faltered before snapping back into place. "None of your business," he barked. "Always snooping. You're paranoid, Taryn."

Taryn's breath caught. The same script, the same gaslighting. But this time, something *cracked* inside her. The old shame and guilt didn't flood in the way they usually did. Instead, she felt... clarity.

This is who he really is, she thought. *No matter how pretty the wrapping, the gift inside never changes.*

She stood, quietly but firmly. "I'm going out."

Pete laughed bitterly. "Of course you are. Storm off like you always do. Maybe ask your little therapy friends what they think."

Taryn didn't take the bait. She grabbed her keys and left without another word.

Michelle's Safe Haven

She found herself on Michelle's doorstep 15 minutes later, tears stinging her eyes before she even knocked. Michelle answered in sweatpants, her face immediately creasing with concern.

"Taryn... what's wrong?"

Taryn burst into tears, falling into Michelle's arms. "It's the *same*, Michelle. It's *always* the same."

Michelle led her inside, guiding her to the couch. Kitty peeked sleepily from the hallway, and Michelle whispered, "Go back to bed, baby." Kitty nodded and disappeared.

Sitting down, Taryn poured it all out—the text message, Pete's anger, the way the facade fell away so quickly. "I feel like such a fool," she whispered.

Michelle shook her head fiercely. "You are *not* a fool. You are brave. Brave for seeing it. Brave for facing it. And brave for coming here instead of shrinking back."

Taryn looked up, tears shining. "I don't know how to *do* this. I don't know how to leave for good."

Michelle squeezed her hand. "You don't have to figure it all out tonight. But this? Right now? You *already started*."

Kyle's Check-In

Meanwhile, Kyle sat on his couch scrolling mindlessly through social media when his phone chimed with a message from Michelle: *"Taryn's here. Rough night. Keep her in your prayers."*

Kyle put his phone down, heart heavy. He stared into the quiet of his apartment and whispered, "Stay strong, Taryn. You've got this."

And he meant it with every fiber of his being.

Group Night: The Breaking Point

At group that week, Taryn looked different. She still sat with her shoulders drawn in, but there was a new light in her eyes—a simmering fire that hadn't been there before.

Marilyn's topic was fitting: *"Recognizing the Breaking Point."*

"There comes a moment," Marilyn began, "when the weight becomes too much, when the cost of staying is greater than the fear of leaving. That's your breaking point—but also, your breakthrough."

Taryn raised her hand slowly. "I think... I hit mine."

The group went silent, every eye on her.

"I've been pretending things were better. Telling myself I could make it work if I just tried harder. But this week... I saw it for what it really is. And I'm done lying to myself."

Her voice wavered but didn't break. "I'm not free yet. But I *will* be."

The room erupted in soft claps and murmurs of support. Marilyn smiled, eyes warm. "That's the beginning of true freedom, Taryn. You've crossed the hardest threshold: seeing the truth and *believing yourself.*"

The affirmation that night: *"I trust myself to choose what is right and good for me."*

Coffee Shop: New Resolve

That night at the coffee shop, the group sat a little closer, talked a little softer. Britney was bubbling with excitement about her new schedule, Kyle was reporting on a peaceful week, and Michelle beamed with quiet pride.

But the focus was Taryn.

She stirred her tea absently, looking up at them. "Thank you for... holding me up. I don't know where I'd be without you."

Michelle leaned forward. "We've *got* you. Every step."

Kyle raised his cup. "To Taryn's courage."

They all clinked mugs, a circle of strength and hope.

Closing Scene: A Quiet Decision

That night, back at home, Taryn sat in her driveway for a long time, staring at the darkened windows of her house. Her fingers traced the steering wheel, heart pounding. Her kids slept quietly in the back seat.

She whispered into the quiet, "One more step."

And with a deep breath, she grabbed their overnight bags—packed and ready—and walked toward the door, determination in every stride.

The road ahead was still uncertain, but Taryn knew one thing for sure:

This time, she wasn't turning back.

Chapter 45

Stepping Into the Unknown

With Kenny and Kate sleeping quietly next to her, Taryn lay awake that night in the quiet of Michelle's guest room, her mind racing even as her body begged for rest. The bag she'd packed sat in the corner—just a duffle, really—but to Taryn, it felt like a suitcase of courage.

She scrolled through her phone, reading old messages from Pete. There they were—the same dizzying pattern: rage, guilt, apology, flattery. She closed her eyes, and the words of Marilyn from group echoed in her mind: *"Seeing the truth and believing yourself is the start of freedom."*

She whispered into the dark, "I believe myself."

And that small declaration felt like a seed being planted.

A New Morning Routine

Michelle's home was a flurry of morning activity—coffee brewing, cartoons playing softly, Kitty, Kate, Kenny and Kevin giggling over cereal. But amid the chaos, there was peace. Taryn sat at the kitchen table, sipping her coffee, marveling at how different life could feel even with small freedoms.

Michelle smiled warmly at her. "It's good to see you breathe."

Taryn smiled back, but it wavered. "It still feels... strange. Like I'm waiting for the hammer to fall."

Michelle nodded. "That's normal. Your nervous system is used to the storm. But the longer you stay out of it, the more you'll realize... peace is real."

Taryn's eyes filled. "I hope so."

Michelle reached over and squeezed her hand. "I know so."

Kyle's Progress

Meanwhile, Kyle was in his own quiet battle. After weeks of staying strong, Natalie had messaged again—this time with nostalgia-laden photos and the familiar pull of guilt-laden apologies.

But Kyle didn't open them. Instead, he texted Michelle: *"Holding the line. No contact. It's hard, but worth it."*

Michelle sent back a simple, proud reply: *"That's huge. I'm so proud of you."*

Kyle smiled, feeling the strength of his own resolve hardening like armor. Then he did something that even shocked himself. He scrolled through his contacts, found Natalie's name and blocked her. Now the temptation to respond would not come knocking when he might be too weak to resist.

Group Night: The Power of Saying No

Marilyn's group that week was packed again. The topic? *"The Power of Saying No."*

"'No' is a full sentence," Marilyn began. "For many of us, we were taught that saying no was rude, selfish, or sinful. But no is a boundary—a life-saving one."

She asked the group to share a recent time they had said no.

Michelle spoke first. "I said no to Matt's request to 'talk things through.' I realized... I didn't owe him that anymore."

Kyle added, "I've been saying no to Natalie's texts. Every time I want to reply... I remind myself why I left."

Taryn was quiet for a long time, then said, "I said no... to myself. To the part of me that wanted to believe Pete had really changed. That's the hardest no I've ever said."

Marilyn beamed. "And one of the most powerful."

The group applauded quietly, everyone feeling the weight of her words.

Britney grinned. "I said no to extra shifts last week. I needed a break."

They all laughed warmly, and the affirmation that night rang true: *"My no protects my peace and power."*

Coffee Shop: Visioning Freedom

Later at the coffee shop, Kyle leaned in, excited. "Okay, question for everyone: If you could do *anything* with your freedom, no limits—what would you do?"

Michelle grinned. "I'd buy a little house with a big garden. Somewhere safe and quiet."

Taryn thought for a long moment. "I think... I'd go back to school. Maybe study counseling. Help women like us."

Kyle's eyes lit up. "That's amazing, Taryn."

Britney chimed in, "I'd travel. Anywhere and everywhere."

They all laughed and dreamed out loud, letting themselves imagine futures that felt big, wild, and *theirs*.

As the evening wound down, Taryn looked around the table, soaking in the warmth of these people who had become her family.

She whispered, "Thank you. For helping me believe in hope again."

Michelle squeezed her hand. "We've got you, Taryn. Always."

A Quiet Night Alone

Back at Michelle's, after everyone was in bed, Taryn stepped out onto the porch, staring up at the moon. She wrapped her arms around herself and took a deep breath.

She felt it—still small, still fragile, but unmistakable.

Freedom.

It was no longer just an idea.

It was becoming a reality.

Chapter 46

The Weight of the Past

Michelle sat at her desk at school, flipping through student essays while sipping her lukewarm coffee. The laughter of her students echoed down the hall, and she allowed herself a moment to breathe it all in—the peace, the normalcy. Her life had become... hers again.

But her phone buzzed—a message from Matt. *"We should talk. For the kids."*

Her stomach clenched. She stared at it, her thumb hovering. Then, with a deep breath, she locked the screen and set it aside.

"No," she whispered to herself. And that was that.

Kyle's Slip

Elsewhere, Kyle stood in line at the grocery store, scrolling his phone out of habit. His eyes caught on Natalie's latest post—her smiling face, holding a cocktail at some beach resort. The caption? *"Healing and growing every day."*

Kyle's chest tightened. *Does she ever even think about me?* he wondered. That old, aching pull tugged at him, but he remembered his pact—with himself, with Michelle and Taryn, with healing.

He put the phone away, paid for his groceries, and left without engaging. It was a small victory, but it felt like a mountain moved.

Taryn's Emotional Rollercoaster

Back at Michelle's house, Taryn was in the guest room folding laundry when her phone rang. Pete. Again.

She let it go to voicemail, but moments later, a message popped up. *"I have news. Please, it's serious."*

Her hands trembled. Against her better judgment, she listened.

Pete's voice was solemn, thick with emotion. "The cancer is back. I need you. I don't know how long I have left."

Taryn's breath hitched, her heart splitting in two. She sank to the bed, staring at the floor, the weight of old love and fresh trauma colliding.

Coffee Shop: The Bombshell

That night at their usual booth, Taryn's face was pale, eyes wide and distant. Michelle and Kyle noticed instantly.

"What's wrong?" Michelle asked gently.

Taryn swallowed hard. "Pete called. He... his cancer is back."

The table fell silent.

Kyle's face tightened. "Are you... are you sure? I mean, you know how he can be..."

Taryn nodded, eyes glassy. "I don't know. I... I feel torn. He's my husband. But... I can't forget everything."

Michelle squeezed her hand. "You don't owe him your *life,* Taryn. Compassion doesn't mean sacrificing yourself all over again."

Taryn's eyes filled with tears. "But how do I *not?* How do I turn my back when someone's dying?"

Kyle was quiet, thoughtful. "It's okay to feel conflicted. It's okay to care. But you have to ask yourself... can you do this without losing *you* again?"

Taryn's breath was ragged. "I don't know."

The affirmation that night at group echoed in her mind: *"My peace matters too."*

Group Night: The Guilt Trap

At group, Marilyn opened with a powerful statement. "Abuse survivors often face deep guilt when the abuser is vulnerable or suffering. But guilt is a tool—one often used to pull you back into unhealthy dynamics. Tonight we'll talk about separating compassion from codependency."

Taryn shared her struggle, her voice shaking. "How do I not feel like a monster for... wanting to keep my distance?"

Marilyn nodded. "It's not wrong to feel compassion. But you must balance it with the reality of your own health and safety. Compassion without boundaries leads to destruction."

Other group members shared similar stories—moments when guilt led them back into harmful situations. The room felt heavy but unified in understanding.

Marilyn closed with, "It's brave to care. It's even braver to care *wisely.*"

The affirmation that night: *"I can care with compassion and still protect my heart."*

A Tense Decision

Back at Michelle's, Taryn lay awake, staring at the ceiling. Her mind was a storm—memories of Pete's cruelty mixed with the haunting sound of his broken voice on the voicemail.

She whispered into the dark, "God, what do I do?"

The silence answered, but deep inside, she felt a stirring—a quiet reminder that the answer wasn't simple, and it wasn't urgent. It was a journey.

She rolled over, hugging her pillow, tears sliding down her cheek. The only thing she knew for sure: whatever came next, she wouldn't face it alone.

Chapter 47

Boundary Set, Boundary Kept

Taryn sat at the kitchen table early the next morning, the house quiet except for the gentle hum of Michelle's coffee maker. Her tea sat untouched as she stared out the window, mind spinning in circles.

Michelle padded in, her hair messy, still in pajamas. "Did you sleep at all?"

Taryn shook her head. "Barely."

Michelle sat across from her. "You're thinking about Pete."

A small nod. "I keep replaying everything. All the times he tore me down... and all the times I stayed. And now... now he's sick again. What if I *don't* go back, and he... dies alone?"

Michelle sighed deeply. "Taryn... it's not your job to save him. He made his choices. You have the right to make yours."

Taryn's eyes brimmed with tears. "I just don't know what's *right*."

Michelle's voice was firm but kind. "What's right is protecting *your peace*."

Kyle's Check-In

Later that day, Taryn met Kyle at the park, needing fresh air and a neutral space. They walked side by side, the late afternoon sun casting long shadows on the path.

"I've been thinking about you," Kyle said gently. "About all of this."

Taryn exhaled shakily. "I feel like I'm failing... again."

Kyle stopped and faced her. "No, you're not. You're *human*. You're wrestling with something huge. But Taryn... don't let guilt write your story. You've come too far."

He paused, eyes serious. "And if you *do* choose to go back, be clear with yourself: know what you're walking into. No illusions. No pretending it's something it's not."

Taryn swallowed hard. "I hear you."

Kyle smiled softly. "Whatever happens... we've got your back."

Group Night: When the Road Forks

At group that week, the topic was fitting: *"Facing Life's Forks in the Road."*

Marilyn began, "Sometimes, life forces us to make choices that feel impossible. But even when the options are painful, the power lies in knowing the choice is yours."

Taryn shared her dilemma with the group, her voice breaking at times but full of honesty.

"I don't want to go back. But... I don't know if I can live with myself if I don't help."

The group listened with compassion. Rachel offered softly, "You can help... without *sacrificing* yourself. There's a difference."

Aaron added, "Sometimes what feels like love... is just old guilt in disguise."

Marilyn smiled. "And sometimes... loving yourself enough to step away is the bravest thing you'll ever do."

The affirmation that night: *"I choose the path that honors my heart and protects my peace."*

The Hardest Call

That night, Taryn stood outside on Michelle's porch, phone in hand, staring at Pete's name on the screen. She finally pressed call.

Pete answered on the first ring. His voice was weak, but familiar. "Taryn."

She took a breath. "I'm sorry you're sick, Pete. I really am. But... I can't come back. I can't go through that again."

A pause. Then Pete's voice, sharp despite his illness: "You're heartless. After everything I've done for you."

Taryn closed her eyes, the familiar words washing over her—but this time, not soaking in.

"No," she said calmly. "You did those things for control, not love. I won't be manipulated anymore. I'll pray for you, Pete. But I'm done."

And she hung up, tears falling, but her spine straight and her heart beating steady.

A Quiet Victory

Inside, Michelle hugged her tightly. "I'm so proud of you."

Taryn smiled through her tears. "I feel... free. And sad. But mostly... free."

They sat in silence, watching the stars blink to life above. The night felt like a new beginning.

And for the first time in a long, long while... Taryn felt like she was finally stepping into her own story.

Chapter 48

A New Light

A week passed, and the weight on Taryn's chest slowly began to lift. She stayed at Michelle's house, still cautious but feeling the edges of hope start to peek through the cracks.

One bright Saturday morning, she woke early and made coffee for the house, the sun pouring through the kitchen windows. She caught a glimpse of herself in the reflection—messy hair, tired eyes—but for the first time in years, she smiled at her own reflection.

Michelle came downstairs, rubbing her eyes. "Look at you, early bird."

Taryn laughed. "Couldn't sleep. But... not because of stress. I feel... peaceful."

Michelle hugged her. "You look lighter."

Taryn exhaled. "I feel it."

Kyle's Growth

Kyle had been quiet that week but not distant. He'd kept busy with work, therapy, and long runs around the lake. He texted the group chat that morning: *"Feeling good today. Want to meet for dinner tonight?"*

Taryn replied first: *"Absolutely."*

Michelle chimed in: *"Count me in."*

It felt good to have something simple and normal to look forward to.

Dinner Out: A Toast to Freedom

That night, the three of them met at a little Italian place with twinkling lights and soft music. The atmosphere felt different this time—lighter, warmer, as though a corner had been turned.

They clinked glasses—water, wine, and sweet tea.

"To freedom," Michelle said softly.

"To friendship," Kyle added.

Taryn raised her glass, her eyes shining. "To new beginnings."

They smiled, each feeling the weight of the moment. They had been through so much together, and now... it felt like they were finally stepping out of the storm.

Britney's Update

As they were finishing dessert, Britney sent a photo to their group chat: a snapshot of her new apartment, tiny but cheerful, with a bright rug and a note: *"First night in my own place! Thank you all for believing in me."*

Michelle beamed. "Look at her. She's thriving."

Kyle laughed. "She's got you as a mentor now, Michelle. She's in good hands."

Taryn smiled. "I'm proud of her. Of all of us."

A Walk Down Memory Lane

After dinner, they walked through the nearby park, reminiscing about their first awkward coffee meetups and the countless tears and laughs shared at that little coffee shop.

"It's wild to think how far we've come," Michelle said.

Taryn nodded. "I honestly didn't think I'd make it out. But here we are."

Kyle looked up at the stars. "We're proof that healing is messy... but possible."

Michelle smiled. "And that we're stronger together."

A Moment of Reflection

That night, alone in her room, Taryn sat at the window, journaling. She wrote about Pete, about the cancer, about guilt, about grace. But mostly, she wrote about herself—her resilience, her growth, her hope.

She closed her journal, whispering to herself, "I am free."

And this time... she truly felt it.

Chapter 49

The Ripples of Change

Spring turned to early summer, and with the longer days came a sense of renewal. Taryn was settling into a rhythm she never thought possible—work, quiet nights, laughter with Michelle and all the kids, and long walks alone where she truly breathed for herself.

One sunny afternoon, Michelle found Taryn in the backyard, planting a small herb garden.

"I'm impressed," Michelle teased, wiping her hands on her jeans. "You've officially claimed your space."

Taryn smiled, brushing dirt from her fingers. "It feels good to grow something... to nurture something that isn't toxic."

Michelle hugged her from the side. "You're doing amazing."

Taryn looked out over the tiny green sprouts. "For the first time, I feel... safe."

Kyle's Turning Point

Meanwhile, Kyle sat across from Marilyn in a one-on-one session. His eyes were brighter than they'd been in months.

"I'm realizing," he said slowly, "that my pattern isn't just about the women I choose. It's about me not believing I deserve better."

Marilyn nodded. "That's powerful insight."

"I've been journaling," Kyle continued. "Listing all the ways I've accepted crumbs when I deserved a feast."

"And what do you want now?" Marilyn asked.

Kyle looked up, eyes clear. "I want peace. Wholeness. And love that doesn't make me small."

Marilyn smiled warmly. "You're on your way."

A Letter from Pete

That evening, Taryn checked the mailbox and found a letter addressed in Pete's handwriting. Her stomach flipped as she carried it inside.

She sat at the table, staring at it for a long time before finally opening it. The letter was surprisingly short.

Taryn,
Thank you for everything you've done. I'm sorry for my mistakes. I don't expect anything, but I wanted to say... you were always stronger than I gave you credit for.
—Pete

Taryn blinked, reading it twice. She didn't cry, didn't shake. She simply folded it, placed it in her journal, and whispered, "Thank you for confirming what I already knew."

She felt... done.

Celebration at the Coffee Shop

That weekend, the group met at their familiar coffee spot, this time joined by Britney, beaming and bright-eyed.

They laughed over pie, sipped their drinks, and swapped stories of small victories—new hobbies, new boundaries, new joys.

Britney raised her cup. "To freedom, round two."

Michelle chuckled. "To mentors and mentees."

Kyle grinned. "And to staying single until we're *really* ready."

Taryn laughed. "I'll drink to all of that."

The coffee shop buzzed around them, but in their corner, it felt like a world of its own—a world built on hard-won strength, deep friendship, and unwavering hope.

A Moment Alone

Later that night, Taryn stood on Michelle's porch, gazing at the stars. She thought of her kids, her future, her friends, and even Pete.

She placed a hand over her heart and whispered, "I am whole."

And this time, there was no question, no hesitation—just truth.

Chapter 50

Full Circle

The summer sun was blazing as Taryn packed up the last of her things at Michelle's house. It had been months now—months of healing, of growth, of tears and laughter. But today, she was moving into her own rental home, just a few blocks away.

Michelle helped her carry boxes to the car. "You sure you're ready for this?" she asked with a grin.

Taryn wiped sweat from her brow and smiled back. "More than ready. It's time."

Michelle hugged her fiercely. "I am *so* proud of you."

Taryn's eyes misted. "I couldn't have done any of this without you."

Michelle shook her head. "You *did* do it. I just walked beside you."

They loaded the final box, and with a last wave, Taryn pulled away—her heart full, her future bright.

A New Apartment, A New Beginning

Taryn stood in the doorway of her new place, the keys jingling in her hand. It was a cute little place— three bedrooms. Kenny and Kate were excited to have their own room again. It was perfect— and it was theirs.

She wandered from room to room, imagining how she'd fill it—with soft blankets, cozy lamps, and maybe even some of those herbs she'd been growing.

She set a candle on the counter, lit it, and whispered, "Thank You, God. For bringing me through."

And as the scent of lavender filled the room, she smiled, feeling more at home in her own skin than she had in years.

Kyle's Progress

Elsewhere, Kyle stood at his easel, brush in hand, finishing a bold new painting. It was abstract—deep reds and blues swirling together—and as he stepped back to admire it, he felt something click into place.

He texted Taryn and Michelle a photo of it with the caption: *"Title: Freedom. Thanks for inspiring me."*

Taryn replied: *"It's stunning, Kyle. So proud of you!"*

Michelle added: *"That's going up in our coffee shop corner!"*

Kyle grinned, heart light.

Michelle's Moment

Michelle walked through her classroom, prepping for the new school year. Posters lined the walls, and stacks of freshly sharpened pencils sat on every desk.

She paused by her own desk, placing a framed photo of her kids beside a small card that read: *"Strong women build each other up."*

Her phone buzzed—a message from Britney. *"Thanks again for helping me prep my resume. Fingers crossed for the interview!"*

Michelle smiled. "You've got this," she whispered to herself.

She looked around her bright, welcoming classroom and felt a surge of pride. *This* was her purpose now—nurturing, teaching, and showing others that freedom was possible.

A Final Gathering

Weeks later, the group met at the coffee shop one last time before the fall rush began. They filled their booth with pie, laughter, and stories.

"I can't believe how far we've come," Britney said, eyes wide.

Taryn nodded. "We've been through the fire—and we're still standing."

Kyle raised his cup. "To the strongest group I've ever known."

They clinked glasses, the sound crisp and full of meaning.

Closing Reflection

That night, Taryn sat alone in her new home, a soft breeze floating through the open window. She opened her journal, flipping back through months of pain, growth, and hard-won wisdom, and

smiled.
She picked up her pen and wrote:

"There was a time I believed I'd never break free. But today, I stand tall—not because it was easy, but because I chose to fight for myself. And that... is the greatest victory of all."

She set the journal down, blew out the candle, and curled up beneath her blanket.
In the quiet of her own safe space, Taryn whispered into the stillness:

"I am home."

And so she rejoiced. And so she healed. Until she truly lived.

Epilogue

Months had passed since the last group meeting, and the seasons had shifted outside Taryn's window. She sat quietly in her home, sunlight spilling across the table, a steaming mug of tea cradled in her hands.

Her life was not perfect—not even close. There were still hard days, moments when old doubts whispered at the edges of her mind, and memories that sometimes surfaced without warning. But there was something new inside her now: space. Space to breathe. Space to heal. Space to begin again.

Michelle was thriving—happily settled in her own apartment, back in the classroom, her laughter coming easier and brighter. Kyle, still learning, was navigating his own journey, still figuring out his patterns and longing for something deeper. Britney was blossoming slowly, finding her footing, standing taller with each new step.

And Taryn?

Taryn had finally chosen herself. She had chosen peace over chaos, truth over appearances, and healing over hiding. She no longer defined herself by what she had survived, but by *who she was becoming*.

She smiled faintly, setting down her mug and opening her journal.

She wrote:

"This is not the end.
This is the beginning of the life I was always meant to live.
I am not what happened to me. I am what I choose to become.
And for the first time in a long time, I am free."

Outside her window, the world stirred with quiet life. And Taryn, heart open and soul steady, stepped forward into a future she had reclaimed—one brave, beautiful step at a time.

Other Books by This Author

I Have to Call Someone Mama

A Grandmother's Story of two Siblings Rescued from Munchausen by Proxy Abuse

The Heart of the Father Series:

A devotional journey of emotional healing and spiritual restoration

1. The God Who Sees
   Healing the Hidden Wounds of Narcissistic Abuse

2. The God Who Heals
   Walking Through Deeper Layers of Emotional Restoration

3. The God Who Loves
   Unfailing Love That Stays When Others Leave

4. The God Who Redeems
   Finding Beauty in the Ashes of Your Story

5. The God Who Restores
   Mending What Was Broken with Tenderness and Truth

6. The God Who Rescues
   From Darkness to Light—Held by Mighty Hands

7. The God Who Strengthens
Learning to Stand Again in the Power of His Love

8. The God Who Comforts
When Your Soul Needs the Softness of His Mercy

9. The God Who Delivers
Breaking the Chains of Shame, Fear, and Control

10. The God Who Never Fails
Anchored in a Love That Cannot Be Shaken

11. The God Who Rebuilds
Step by Step, Reclaiming the Ruins with Grace

12. The God Who Will Never Leave You or Forsake You
Held Forever in the Heart of the Father

For Immediate Help (U.S.)

National Suicide & Crisis Lifeline
Call or text **988**
Visit: 988lifeline.org
24/7, free, confidential support for anyone in emotional distress or suicidal crisis.

National Domestic Violence Hotline
Call **800-799-7233 (SAFE)**
Text **START** to **88788**
Visit: thehotline.org
24/7 support, safety planning, and local resources for anyone experiencing domestic abuse.

RAINN (Rape, Abuse & Incest National Network)
Call **800-656-HOPE (4673)**
Visit: rainn.org
Confidential support for survivors of sexual assault and abuse.